Presidential Campaigns in the Age of Social Media

This book is part of the Peter Lang Political Science, Economics, and Law list.
Every volume is peer reviewed and meets
the highest quality standards for content and production.

PETER LANG
New York • Bern • Berlin
Brussels • Vienna • Oxford • Warsaw

William L. Benoit and Mark J. Glantz

Presidential Campaigns in the Age of Social Media

Clinton and Trump

PETER LANG
New York • Bern • Berlin
Brussels • Vienna • Oxford • Warsaw

Library of Congress Cataloging-in-Publication Data

Names: Benoit, William L., author. | Glantz, Mark J. author.
Title: Presidential campaigns in the age of social media: Clinton and Trump / William L. Benoit and Mark J. Glantz.
Description: New York: Peter Lang, 2019.
Includes bibliographical references and index.
Identifiers: LCCN 2019017741 | ISBN 978-1-4331-6822-2 (hardback: alk. paper)
ISBN 978-1-4331-6823-9 (ebook pdf)
ISBN 978-1-4331-6824-6 (epub) | ISBN 978-1-4331-6825-3 (mobi)
Subjects: LCSH: Presidents—United States—Election—1992. | Presidents—United States—Election—1996. | Presidents—United States—Election—2016. | Communication in politics—United States. | Political campaigns—Technological innovations—United States. | Social Media—Political aspects—United States. | Mass media—Political aspects—United States. | Clinton, Bill, 1946– | Trump, Donald, 1946–
Classification: LCC JK526 1992 .B46 2019 | DDC 324.7/3097309049—dc23
LC record available at https://lccn.loc.gov/2019017741
DOI 10.3726/b16098

Bibliographic information published by **Die Deutsche Nationalbibliothek.**
Die Deutsche Nationalbibliothek lists this publication in the "Deutsche Nationalbibliografie"; detailed bibliographic data are available on the Internet at http://dnb.d-nb.de/.

29 Broadway, 18th floor, New York, NY 10006
www.peterlang.com

Table of Contents

Preface

The 2016 presidential race was highly unusual in a variety of ways. For example, Donald Trump relied less on TV spots, and more on social media, than candidates in previous races. The candidates in 2016—Hillary Clinton and Donald Trump—were the two least popular presidential candidates for as long as this variable has been measured (Collins, 2016). The electorate has also shifted over time: most voters now dislike the opposing party more than they like their own party (Abramowitz & Webster, 2016, 2018), giving candidates more incentive to attack than in previous years. As in the 2000 presidential election, the candidate who won the popular vote was not the candidate who won the Electoral College (this situation also occurred twice in the 1800s), although in 2016 Donald Trump won the Electoral College while losing the popular vote by millions of votes (Kreig, 2016), more than five times the number as in 2000. Voters have differences in their beliefs, values, and attitudes (Fishbein & Ajzen, 2010), which means they do not all react the same way to a given message. Nevertheless, considerable evidence confirms that election campaign messages have significant effects on voters. A meta-analysis of the effects of watching election debates on voters found that these events increase voters' knowledge of the candidates' issue positions, agenda-setting, perceptions of the candidates' character, vote preference; these effects are even larger for primary debates than general election debates (Benoit, Hansen, & Verser, 2003). Meta-analysis of the effects of TV spot on voters found that these messages increase issue knowledge, affect perceptions of the candidates' character, influenced agenda-setting, and affected voter turnout (Benoit, Leshner, & Chattopadhyay, 2007). Reinemann and Maurer (2005) showed that viewers react differently to acclaims and attacks in debate messages. Research also established that topic of campaign messages have effects: Candidates who stress policy more than their opponents (and character less) were significantly more likely to win elections (Benoit, 2003). Election campaign messages are clearly capable of influencing voters.

In 2016, Hillary Clinton was well-known; she had served as First Lady, Senator from New York, Democratic presidential primary candidate, and Secretary of State. On the other hand, Donald Trump had never served in elective office so he had no public political record for voters to consider. Nor was it easy for voters to infer his political positions from his political party affiliation. He declared he was a Republican in 1987, switched to the Independence Party of New York in 2001, said he was a Democrat in 2009, changed to the Republican Party, registered as an independent, and in 2012 he registered again as a Republican (Political positions of Donald Trump, 2018). Of course, he was known as a real estate magnate and television personality. It is difficult to imagine that primary and general election messages (speeches, debates, ads, tweets, and so forth) did not help voters learn about Donald Trump as a presidential candidate or influence their attitudes toward him. There is no doubt that this presidential campaign deserves scholarly attention.

Previous research has established baselines for select aspects of the content of presidential campaign messages such as primary and general TV spots, primary and general debates, or primary (announcement) and general (acceptance) speeches (see, e.g., Benoit, 2007). Research has started to apply Functional Theory to social media: 2012 Facebook posts (Shen & Benoit, 2016); 2016 gubernatorial, senate, and house tweets in 2016 (Benoit & Stein, 2018). With the emergence of social media as a key medium of communication in 2016, content analysis of candidate messages on Twitter and Facebook in particular deserves scrutiny. This book will add to our understanding of this watershed election while comparing the content of new social media to that in more traditional media.

Bill would like to thank his family, Pamela J. Benoit and Jennifer M. Benoit-Bryan, for their continuing support. I also appreciate Mark's excellent work on our book. Mark would like to thank his partner Amy, his tall son Charlie, and his colleagues at St. Norbert College. Bill and Mark would like to thank Professor Todd Holm for permission to reprint the article reporting a meta-analysis of Functional Theory from *Speaker & Gavel.*

CHAPTER ONE

Introduction

Considering the prominence of the United States in the world today, as well as the size and complexity of the U.S. itself, the occupant of the Oval Office is extremely important, the most powerful elected official in the world. He or she leads America's foreign policy—including our national defense, trade with other countries, and foreign aid—and administers a federal government that oversees an ever-increasing population and incredibly complex domestic policies. Accordingly, any presidential election merits scholarly attention, including the one conducted in 2016.

However, the 2016 presidential campaign in particular deserves our careful consideration. Regardless of which candidate, or whose policies, one embraces, there is no doubt whatsoever that President Donald Trump advanced far different policies and enacted a much different persona than Hillary Clinton would have if she had won the Electoral College in 2016. This election dramatically underscores that presidential elections matter greatly to our country and the importance of studying these quadrennial events.

No two presidential elections are exactly the same. The nominees change from election to election; even candidates who run more than once (such as Ronald Reagan, Bill Clinton, George W. Bush or Barack Obama) are not exactly the same (same persona, same policies) the second time around, when they sought re-election, as they were in their initial run. For example, incumbent candidates can boast of a record in the office being contested and be criticized for their record in the Oval Office, unlike challengers. This feature guarantees that candidates who win an initial term in the White House will run a different campaign when seeking re-election. Furthermore, the electorate changes every four years as some voters pass away or stop participating in elections and new citizens reach voting age. The issues that matter most to voters change from one election to another. For example, joblessness or inflation may become more or less important to voters as perceptions of the economy shift. Some voters' policy preferences shift over time and they react to newly emergent problems and situations. For example, the horrific events of 9/11 changed how voters and candidates felt about terrorism. Candidates running for office in 2000 (or before) had no reason to present plans to deal with the kind of terrorism that flew highjacked airplanes into buildings—but in 2004 and beyond this was an issue that needed to be addressed in campaigns. The media available for candidates to use to reach voters evolves over time (e.g., from radio to television to webpages to social media). However, in the midst of this diversity one could argue that the 2016 presidential campaign was particularly unusual, sharply distinct from earlier contests.

In 2016 neither major party nominee was the sitting president or vice president (Vice President Joe Biden declined to run). In modern history this situation had occurred only in 1952 and 2000. Other differences between 2016 and other presidential elections can be identified as well. No candidate had ever relied on social media as much, or as effectively, as Donald Trump did in this campaign. Partly because of his use of social media and his penchant for attracting media attention through behavior many considered outrageous, total spending on presidential television advertising dropped for the first time in recent history (still, $2.4 billion dollars were spent on the 2016 presidential primary and general election campaigns; Ingraham, 2017). On the other hand, spending on digital media increased $1.2 billion from 2012 (Borrell Associates, 2017). When former First Lady, Senator, and Secretary of State Hillary Clinton won the Democratic nomination she became the first woman selected as the presidential nominee of a major party. Other women, such as Geraldine Ferraro and Sarah Palin, had served as major party vice presidential candidates but never in history had a woman received the Democratic or Republican nomination for president. Furthermore, presidential candidates without previous experience in office are quite rare. One of the relatively successful third party candidates in recent history, business magnate H. Ross Perot, who had no elective experience, lost the his two bids for the presidency. Even actor Ronald Reagan had served as governor of California before he ran for president. Donald Trump managed to win both the Republican nomination and the Electoral College without any prior experience in elective office. Having no experience as a politician, Trump repeatedly boasted of his superb management experience in business (although he curiously he refused to release his tax returns to show how wealthy he was). He capitalized on his circumstances by running as an outsider and claiming his primary campaign was self-funded (see Carroll, 2016). Another difference is the growing partisan divide in America. Davenport (2017) explained that "as recently as the early 1970s, party unity voting was around 60% but today it is closer to 90% in both the House and Senate." This polarized environment was another important factor in the 2016 elections.

Expectations were toppled in the 2016 presidential campaign. Commentators thought "Jeb Bush would take the Republican presidential nomination" (Kaye, 2017). In contrast, Donald Trump was not the favorite when he entered the race on June 16, 2015. In fact, a public opinion poll from that month put Jeb Bush at 22% and Trump at 1% (Todd & Murray, 2015). In September pollster Nate Silver concluded that Donald Trump was not likely to win the Republican nomination (Tani, 2015). Clinton did secure her party's nomination, as expected, but no one anticipated Bernie Sanders' surprisingly strong primary challenge. In October odds makers gave Hillary Clinton the nod, concluding that her chances of winning the presidency were far better than any other candidate, and over seven times as likely as Trump. However, Trump confounded almost everyone by winning the GOP nomination in the primary campaign and the Electoral College in the general campaign (although he lost the popular vote by nearly three million votes; Kreig, 2016).

Trump's campaign style was also unprecedented. He broke with tradition by spending less on television spots than recent presidential candidates. A report issued by Borrell Associates observed that "The 2016 presidential campaign proved, for the first time, that a candidate doesn't have to match or outspend an opponent in TV commercials—or even in overall funds raised—to win an election" (Kaye, 2017). Instead of spending vast sums on TV spots, Trump relied heavily on social media and coverage in the news media to reach voters. Brad Parscale, who ran Trump's digital campaign in 2016, observed that "Twitter is how he [Trump] talked to the people. Facebook was going to be how he won" (60 Minutes, 2017). The business magnate also freely insulted his opponents, giving them derogatory nicknames such as "Lyin' Ted" Cruz, "Little Marco" Rubio, or "Crooked Hillary" Clinton. Clearly, the 2016 American presidential election deserves study.

The 2016 campaign also merits scholarly inquiry because of the extremely close outcome. Clinton won the popular vote by almost three million votes (Abramson, 2016) but Trump took the Electoral College by 306 to 232 (270 votes are needed to win). Even the Electoral College outcome was closer than it appears. Had only 38,872 voters switched from Trump to Clinton in three battleground states

(Pennsylvania, Michigan, and Wisconsin) Clinton would have won the Electoral College as well as the popular vote (or, if 78,000 Democrats who stayed home had actually gone to the polls in these states and voted for Clinton, the Democrat would have won; or if 78,000 fewer Trump voters had actually cast votes he would have lost the Electoral College, *The Economist*, 2016). Trump's margin of victory was razor thin when over 130 million votes were cast in this election (this narrow victory could well be why President Trump so grudgingly accepts the intelligence community's conclusions of Russian meddling in the election: His win could be seen to be a result of Russian meddling rather than his own appeal to voters). It is difficult to deny that campaign messages are vitally important in these circumstances.

A final reason to study the 2016 presidential campaign concerns the Democratic and Republican nominees. Collins (2016) explained that "Donald Trump and Hillary Clinton are the two most unpopular presidential candidates in more than 30 years of ABC News/*Washington Post* polling.... With registered voters, the two are basically tied: Clinton has 59% unfavorability and Trump has 60%." This was a campaign like no other.

This study investigates the 2016 presidential campaign using the Functional Theory of Political Campaign Discourse (Benoit, 2007). Functional Theory cannot provide answers to all possible questions—no theory of election messages can do so—but it does answer useful questions about functions and topics of these messages. Furthermore, longitudinal studies of a variety of message forms (such as announcement speeches, acceptance addresses, TV spots, debates; Benoit, 2007) provide an important context for understanding the 2016 presidential campaign. This study also provides insight into the relatively new campaign medium of social media.

Functional Theory of Political Campaign Discourse

Some research into political campaigns is a-theoretical. A number of studies identify two functions—positive (acclaims) and negative (attacks) without consideration of defenses (defenses are particularly important for research on election debates, but occur in other media as well). These two dimensions are found most frequently in research on political TV spots (Benoit, 2014a). Functional Theory offers a theoretical perspective on functional and topics of political campaign messages, elucidated in Chapter 2. It also offers several important advantages to researchers. Content analysis of campaign messages most often focuses on TV spots; research driven by Functional Theory has investigated a variety of campaign media such as debates, candidacy announcement speeches, nomination acceptance addresses, direct mail advertising, candidate web-pages, candidate press releases, talk radio appearances, television talk show appearances, and social media (see Benoit, 2007). Functional Theory has developed longitudinal data bases on several message forms, such as primary TV spots and debates, announcement and acceptance speeches, primary and general direct mail brochures, primary and general debates and has examined messages in campaigns for other offices and in other countries.

Content analysis of TV spots usually adopts the entire spot as the coding unit despite the fact than many individual ads use *both* acclaims and attacks (and occasionally defenses) and address *both* policy and character (usually called issues and images). The proportion of functions and topics varies across spots; we cannot assume, for example, that policy and character each comprise 50% of a given ad. Accordingly, coding the entire spot is therefore less accurate than content analysis using themes or arguments as the coding unit (see, e.g., Benoit, 2017a). Nor is the entire spot an appropriate coding unit for such media as speeches, candidate web-pages, or debates and therefore cannot produce comparable data for other media besides spots. Would one use the entire speech as a coding unit when analyzing acceptance addresses? Additionally, other research on campaign messages rarely delves deeper than policy (issue) and character (image); Functional Theory divides each of these topics into three sub-forms (policy is divided into remarks on past deeds, [specific] future plans, and general goals; character consists of comments on personal qualities of the candidate, the candidate's leadership ability, and the candidate's ideals). Functional Theory also investigates target of attack in primary campaigns, answering the question of whether candidates focus most of their criticism on members of their own party or on members of the opposition party. Functional Theory has also investigated the effect on source (candidate- versus party- or group-sponsored TV spots) on functions of campaign messages.

Evidence exists to support both the reliability and validity of data gathered using Functional Theory. Some research into political campaign discourse does not report inter-coder reliability (see Benoit, 2017 for examples); it is not possible to assess the reliability of such data. Reliability of data developed using Functional Theory is strong. Cohen's κ for Functional data ranges from .75 to 1.0 (see Benoit, 2017); Landis and Koch (1977) state that values of κ from .61 to .80 reflect "substantial agreement and values from 0.81 to 1.0 indicate 'almost perfect'" inter-coder reliability. Furthermore, Geer (2006) argues that his data should be considered valid because his measure of negativity "correlates… a staggering 0.97 with Benoit's" measure of attacks (p. 36). Of course, this also means that Geer's data provide evidence of the validity of Functional data. Finally, Functional Theory offers many examples of the concepts employed in this theory, providing face validity (see, e.g., Benoit, 2017a).

Functional Theory has received increasing acceptance in the literature on political campaigns. Nai and Walter (2015) edited a book on negative campaigning, adopting Functional Theory "as a baseline for defining and measuring negative campaigning" (p. 17). Hrbkova and Zagrapan (2014) noted that "The most influential attempt at systematic analysis of political debates based on a specific theoretical concept is the Functional Theory" (p. 736). Isolatus (2011) observed that "One of the most used and systematically tested theories in the studies of the content of television debates has been Functional Theory" (p. 31). Furthermore, meta-analysis has confirmed predictions derived from Functional Theory (Benoit, 2017). Use of Functional Theory for a study of 2016 presidential campaign messages is well-justified.

Candidates produce a plethora of campaign messages, posters, direct mail brochures, TV spots (and ads on radio and the Internet), debates, TV show interviews, emails, candidate webpages, yard signs, and, recently, social media such as Twitter and Facebook. Rather than try to locate and analyze every candidate election medium, we chose a very traditional message form, speeches (candidacy announcements and nomination acceptances), two media which rose to prominence over about four decades, television and televised debates, primary television talk show appearances (apparently neither Clinton nor Trump used this medium in the general campaign), along with the recently developed social media (Twitter and Facebook). These choices offer both a manageable data collection and analysis task and an important cross-section of presidential campaign discourse.

This research deploys content analysis based on the Functional Theory of Political Campaign Discourse using the procedures developed for this research (see, e.g., Benoit, Blaney, & Pier, 1998; Benoit, McHale, Hansen, Pier, & McGuire, 2003; Benoit, Stein, McHale, Chattopadhyay, Verser, & Price, 2007; as well as Benoit, 2014a, 2014c or Benoit, Pier, Brazeal, McHale, Klyukovksi, & Airne, 2002). Using a common method allows comparisons among these media from 2016 and between candidate messages from 2016 and prior campaigns. Chapter 2 outlines the method and procedures employed here. The following eight chapters investigate candidate messages in the media just mentioned. A final chapter undertakes comparisons and draws conclusions.

2016 Presidential Candidacies

Eleven people actively sought the Republican presidential nomination. The candidates are listed by announcement date; the dates candidates withdrew from the campaign are also provided. We do not possess texts for every candidate in every message form; for example, some declared candidates did not participate in debates or appear on TV talk shows.

Ted Cruz March 23, 2015–May 3, 2016
Rand Paul April 7, 2015–February 3, 2016
Marco Rubio April 13, 2015–March 15, 2016
Ben Carson May 3, 2015–March 4, 2016
Carly Fiorina May 4, 2015–February 10, 2016
Mike Huckabee May 5, 2015–February 1, 2016
George Pataki May 28, 2015–December 29, 2015
Lindsey Graham June 1, 2015–December 21, 2015
Rich Perry June 4, 2015–September 4, 2015
Jeb Bush June 15, 2015–February 20, 2016
Donald Trump June 15, 2015–clinched nomination July 2016
Bobby Jindal June 24, 2015–November 17, 2015
Rick Santorum May 27, 2015–February 3, 2016
Chris Christie June 30, 2015–February 10, 2016
Scott Walker July 13, 2015–September 21, 2015
John Kasich July 21, 2015–May 4, 2016

Five candidates actively contested the Democratic presidential nomination. Again, these candidates are listed by date of their announcement with withdrawal date mentioned. Again, we do not have texts for these five candidates for all message forms we investigate.

Hillary Clinton April 12, 2015–clinched nomination July 2016
Bernie Sanders April 30, 2015–June 12, 2016
Martin O'Malley May 30, 2015–February 1, 2016
Lincoln Chafee June 3, 2015–October 23, 2015
Jim Webb July 2, 2015–October 30, 2015

As noted, this study does not have data on all of these candidates for all message forms. However, the people we consider to be the major candidates are represented throughout.

CHAPTER TWO

Methods and Procedures

The Functional Theory of Political Campaign Discourse was developed in 1999 to study presidential nomination acceptance addresses (Benoit, Wells, Pier, & Blaney, 1999). It has been employed to understand presidential primary and general TV spots from 1952 to 2012 (Benoit, 2014a), presidential primary and general debates (including vice presidential debates; Benoit, 2014c), presidential candidacy announcement speeches (Benoit, Henson, Whalen, & Pier, 2008) and other presidential and non-presidential campaign messages, including messages from non-U.S. elections (Benoit, 2007). This chapter discusses the assumptions of this theory, predictions and research questions developed for it, and the procedures employed for analyzing 2016 presidential campaign messages.

Assumptions of Functional Theory

This approach to political campaign communication relies on five important assumptions about election campaigns (Benoit, 2007). First, Functional Theory notes that voting is a comparative act. In order to win a political election, candidates need only accomplish one basic goal: they need to appear preferable to their opponents—and we must keep in mind what matters most in political campaigns are voters' perceptions. It is not necessary for a candidate to persuade all voters of their superiority; they must only persuade enough voters to win the election. This is important because many political issues are controversial and people disagree about the most important character traits of a president. Today's political environment is highly polarized; recall how many votes in congress are now made along party lines. A candidate who espouses a specific position on any controversial issue is certain to simultaneously attract and repel different groups of voters with different beliefs and values on that issue. The remaining assumptions make it clear why communication is vital to political election campaigns.

A second assumption is that candidates for elective offices have to draw some contrasts between themselves and their opponent(s). Those who seek political office need not disagree with opponents on every question. For example, who would oppose curbing inflation, creating jobs, or protecting the country from terrorists (of course, substantial disagreements exist about *how* to achieve these goals)? However, without the existence of some differences between or among candidates voters would have no reason to prefer one candidate over another.

Third, citizens obtain information about candidates and their issue stands through election messages from a variety of sources, including candidates, their adherents, the news media, and special interest groups. The rise of the Internet and social media such as Twitter and Facebook increases exponentially the amount of information available to voters. Candidates use messages in a variety of media to inform voters about their character and policy positions (and to establish differences between themselves and opponents), including TV spots, debates, speeches, webpages, social media, and TV talk shows. In the 2016 campaign, for example, Donald Trump made headlines repeatedly with controversial tweets which distinguished him from his opponents.

Having identified some differences between themselves and their opponents, candidates for elective office must establish their preferability to opponents. For example, political candidates who declared "I believe employment is too high and I will reduce it if elected" would clearly differentiate themselves from their opponents, but not in a way that would endear them to voters. Candidates must identify differences that make them *appear* superior to opponents. They establish preferability by using messages that employ the three functions of acclaims, attacks, and defenses. Acclaims are statements that promote candidates' strengths or advantages. Attacks, in contrast, identify opponents' alleged weaknesses or disadvantages. Defenses are remarks that respond to, or refute, attacks made against candidates. These three functions work together in a way that can be likened to an informal version of cost-benefit analysis. This observation does not mean Functional Theory assumes that voters quantify benefits (acclaims) or costs (attacks and defenses) or that they engage in mathematical calculations (adding or averaging costs and benefits) to make vote choices. Acclaims are capable of increasing a candidate's perceived benefits. Attacks can increase the apparent costs of an opponent. Defenses have the potential to reduce a candidate's perceived costs. Functional Theory does not assume that acclaims, attacks, and defenses are necessarily persuasive: Some messages are poorly conceived or do not reach the intended audience; some voters are far from open-minded. Our currently polarized environment means that no candidate could obtain support from all voters; luckily one need not persuade everyone to win an election. Furthermore, the existing knowledge about and attitudes toward candidates of voters varies, as does the way citizens perceive messages from and about candidates (Jarman, 2005, showed that debate viewers tend to evaluate their preferred candidates more favorably than opposing candidates).

Campaign messages can discuss two topics, policy and character, a fifth assumption of Functional Theory. Candidates can acclaim, attack, and defend (1) what he or she has done or will do in office (policy) and (2) the kind of person he or she is (character). Rountree (1995) distinguishes between *actus* or *what we do* and *status* (nature) or *who we are* in political discourse. Traditional research often refers to these two topics as "issue" and "image." However, the terms "policy" and "character" are preferable to other terms often encountered in the literature. The term "issue" refers to disputable questions. Because candidates often discuss their personalities, it is possible for character to be an issue (a disputable question) in a campaign. Furthermore citizens develop perceptions—impressions or images—of the candidates' policy positions as well as their character, which means one could talk about voters' "images" of their policy positions. Using the terms "policy" and "character" avoids these potential difficulties.

We must realize that these two topics have some overlap. When a candidate takes a particular policy position that could well influence the audience's perceptions of that candidate's character. For example, proposing a plan to help the poor (a policy) could foster the impression that the candidate is compassionate (a character trait). Similarly, if a voter thinks a candidate is a bigot (a character trait) that voter might well assume this candidate would oppose legislation to help minorities (a policy). Still, legislation to help the poor or minorities is clearly different from the personal qualities of compassion or bigotry. High values for inter-coder reliability in research using the Functional approach on topics of campaign discourse, mentioned in the previous chapter, demonstrates that despite some possible overlap, policy and character are distinct topics.

Functional Theory further divides discourse on policy into three sub-forms: past deeds (record in office), future plans (means or specific proposals for policy), and general goals (ends, desired future state of affairs). Functional Theory focuses on the past (past deeds) and the future (future plans and general goals). It does not, however, have a category to represent campaign discourse using the present tense. For example, candidates sometimes make statements like "I am working hard to lower taxes." If this work has actually reduced taxes, that accomplishment should be (and almost certainly would be) used as the basis for an acclaim on past deeds (e.g., "Taxes decreased increased 15% under my leadership"). On the other hand, if that hard work has not yet produced lower taxes, the statement is essentially an acclaim on general goals ("My goal is reducing taxes"). This analysis comports well with theories of voting from political science which identify two theories of vote choice: Retrospective voting, where vote choice is based on an assessment of what the candidates have accomplished in the past, versus prospective voting, which bases vote choice on speculation about what the candidates will likely accomplish (in the future) if elected (Lanoue, 1994; see also Benoit, 2006). No competing theory of voting based on the present tense has been put forward.

Functional Theory also sub-divides discourse on character into remarks about personal qualities (personality), leadership ability (experience in elective office, ability to lead), and ideals (values or principles). Appendix 2.1 provides multiple illustrative examples of acclaims and attacks on each form of policy and character taken from the 2016 presidential campaign (most Functional studies include similar appendices illustrating acclaims and attacks on the forms of policy and character). One set of examples provided here is taken from the primary (Hillary Clinton's twitter feed), another is from the general election (Donald Trump's Facebook page), and a third set of examples is taken from the general presidential debates. These examples illustrate the coding system applied here and provide face validity to the coding reported here (the examples provided in the presentation of results provide additional evidence for face validity).

Functional Theory has held up well in research. A meta-analysis of research on this approach confirmed several predictions from Functional Theory. The Appendix reprints this study and helps understand the method employed here.

Hypotheses and Research Questions

Eight hypotheses will be tested with data from the 2016 campaign; three research questions will also be answered with these data. The first prediction concerns the functions of campaign messages. Acclaims have no inherent disadvantages, attacks have one potential drawback (many voters dislike mudslinging, so an attack can generate backlash—see, e.g., Merritt, 1984; Stewart, 1975), and defenses have three limitations (defenses can make a candidate appear reactive rather than proactive; because attacks usually address the target's weaknesses, defenses often take a candidate off message; one must identify an attack in order to refute it, so a defense can inform or remind voters of a potential weakness). So, candidates have reasons to use more acclaims than attacks and more attacks than defenses. Functional Theory predicts:

> H1. Acclaims will be more common than attacks, which in turn will be more common than defenses.

Functional Theory does not posit that acclaims are necessarily more persuasive than attacks, just that they are likely to occur more frequently than attacks. Furthermore, this theory does not assert that candidates *must* acclaim more than they attack, only that they have reasons to do so. Some candidates may not fully appreciate the dangers of backlash against mudslinging. Some candidates may hate their opponents so much they cannot refrain from attacking. Some candidates may be such nasty people their vitriol pervades the campaign messages they spout. Still, candidates have reasons to acclaim more than they attack and in fact most candidates do so (see, e.g., Benoit, 2007). Similarly, defenses, with the three drawbacks identified above, are the least likely function.

It is important to acknowledge that attacks are not necessarily false or misleading (Benoit, 2013): Some attacks are reasonable just as some acclaims are not. Geer (2006) argues that informed decision making requires an understanding of both pros and cons, so attacks can be an important part of the democratic process. He also notes that attacks are more likely to include evidence than acclaims.

Some citizens think the most important function of a president is to serve as a role model (character) but more voters see the most important factor in evaluating political leaders is their work proposing and implementing governmental policy. Public opinion polls in the U.S. reveals that more respondents say policy is a more important determinant for their vote for president than character (Benoit, 2003). Benoit also contrasted the topics of candidates who won (primary, acceptance, general; primary and general TV spots and debates, acceptance addresses): Winners were significantly more likely to discuss policy, and less likely to discuss character, than losers. Hofstetter (1976) wrote that "issue preferences are key elements in the preferences of most, if not all, voters" (p. 77). King (2002) analyzed studies on the role of character in 51 elections held in 6 countries between 1960 and 2001 confirming that "It is quite unusual for leaders' and candidates' personality and other personal traits to determine election outcomes" (p. 216). So, policy is more important than character in the outcome of elections. Candidates know voters' preferences so Functional Theory predicts:

> H2. Policy will be more common than character.

As with functions, this theory does not declare that candidates *must* discuss policy more than character, only that they have reasons to do so. Some candidates are exceptions, but research confirms this prediction with many American political campaign messages (see Benoit, 2007, 2014a, 2014c). Baker and Norpoth's (1981) analysis of the 1972 West German debates found that candidates discussed issues (policy) more than ethics (character), consistent with this prediction.

One variable that has been studied in some research on presidential primary campaigns is target of attack. In the general election major party nominees have no choice about whom to attack: their opposite number. However, in the primary campaign candidates can attack their immediate opponents in the primary election—candidates from their own party—or their potential opponents—candidates from the other party whom they might face in the general election. These two targets of attack are quite different. Attacking either kind of target has the potential to reduce the target's desirability. However, attacking a member of the opposing party during the primary could tend to serve as a kind of acclaim. For example, in the 2016 presidential primary, when candidate Donald Trump attacked Hillary Clinton or Barack Obama, Republicans may have liked Trump more than if he had remained silent. By the same token, when Hillary Clinton or Bernie Sanders attacked Donald Trump in the Democratic primary, their supporters may have become even more energized on behalf of the attacker. So, attacking one's opponent in the primary or the general election can damage the target. But attacking the other party in the primary can enhance the source of attacks.

The potential for backlash from attacks (voters profess to dislike mudslinging: Merritt, 1984; Stewart, 1975) also varies by target. To win the nomination, for instance, a Republican needs to increase his or her favorability among Republicans. When Trump—or any other Republican primary candidate—attacks a Republican such as Ted Cruz or Marco Rubio in the primary, that risks alienating some Republicans. Some Republican primary voters liked Cruz and Rubio and attacks on them could hurt the attacker. However, attacking Clinton is unlikely to hurt his chances in Republican the primary. Attacks on Clinton could damage Trump later if he wins the Republican nomination (as he did) in the general election, but those who would be most offended probably would not vote for Trump in any event. Of course, candidates usually must attack to some extent in drive down the target's favorability. The point is that attacking different kinds of targets can have different effects.

Target of attack has been studied in several campaigns (this research includes a third possible target of attack, *status quo*, identifying problems). Benoit, Blaney, and Pier (1998) investigated this variable in the 1996 presidential campaign. Benoit et al. (2003) content analyzed messages using this variable in messages from the 2000 campaign for the Oval Office. Benoit et al. (2007) investigated this variable in the 2004 campaign. Presidential primary debates are message form in which target of attack has been studied the most. Benoit et al. (2002) analyzed presidential primary debates from 1948 (a radio debate between two Republicans) through the year 2000.

The 2008 presidential primary debates are investigated in Glantz, Benoit, and Airne (2013); the primary debates from 2012 were studied in Benoit and Glantz (2015). Some message forms/years stressed attacks on the attacker's own party; other message forms/years emphasized attacks on the opposing party. In both parties there was a slight emphasis on attacking other members of one's own party (Democrats did so in 3 of 5 cases; Republicans did this in 4 or 6 cases). Combining all these data, there was a slight preference for attacking one's own party (51%) than attacking the other party (49%) in the primary campaign. Table 2.1 summarizes these data.

RQ1. In the primaries, how often were candidates from the two parties attacked?

As noted earlier, Functional theory divides policy into three forms (past deeds, future plans, general goals) and character into three aspects (personal qualities, leadership ability, ideals). Two additional research questions will also be addressed in this study.

RQ2. What is the proportion of the three forms of policy?

RQ3. What is the proportion of the three forms of character?

Functional Theory offers two predictions about the forms of policy and character. It is easier to for a candidate to embrace (acclaim) general goals and ideals

Table 2.1. Target of Attack in Presidential Primary Campaigns.

Message	Own Party	Other Party
1996, 2000 R primary TV spots	**219 (93%)**	16 (7%)
1996 R primary talk radio	**61 (85%)**	11 (15%)
2000 R primary web pages	9 (12%)	69 (88%)
2000 R radio spots	**103 (71%)**	43 (29%)
2000 R TV talk shows	**119 (83%)**	24 (17%)
1948–2012 R primary debates	1188 (49%)	**1221 (51%)**
Total 1948–2012 R	**1699 (55%)**	1384 (45%)
2000, 2004 D primary TV spots	**49 (62%)**	30 (38%)
2000, 2004 D primary web	45 (10%)	**402 (90%)**
2000, 2004 D primary radio spots	**28 (57%)**	21 (43%)
2000, 2004 D primary TV talk shows	129 (23%)	**440 (77%)**
[illegible]2008 primary debates	**2199 (57%)**	1689 (43%)
[illegible]-2008 D	2450 (49%)	**2582 (51%)**
	4149 (51%)	3966 (49%)

than to reject them (attack). For instance, what candidate would oppose the goal of creating jobs or or keeping America safe? Similarly, candidates are less likely to attack than acclaim when discussing ideals: It is difficult to criticize values and principles such as equal opportunity or justice. This consideration leads to two hypotheses.

> H3. General goals will form the basis for more acclaims than attacks.

> H4. Ideals will form the basis for more acclaims than attacks.

Our sample for TV spots began with ads sponsored by candidates; this choice makes the data reported here comparable with past data on TV spots. However, we also collected and content analyzed TV commercials sponsored by groups. This additional data allows us to test an additional hypothesis with TV Spots:

> H5. TV spots sponsored by candidates use more acclaims, and fewer attacks, than ads sponsored by groups.

Past research has established that ads by candidates are more positive than ads from groups (such as party-sponsored ads or spots ran by groups; Airne & Benoit, 2005). The idea here is that attacks risk a possible backlash; the hope is that when a group makes most of the attacks, the backlash will be deflected to some extent away from the candidates.

Four hypotheses will be tested, and additional research questions answered, with data from all chapters combined (Chapter 11). Functional Theory posits three reasons why defenses are expected to be the least common function: to refute an attack requires you to identify it, which could remind or inform voters of a potential weakness; attacks typically occur on the target's weaknesses, so responding to an attack will usually take the defender off message; and defending could make a candidate appear reactive rather than proactive. However, a candidate who is attacked during a debate need not worry that a defense will remind or inform voters of a potential weakness: viewers just saw and heard the attack. So, Functional Theory predicts that defenses will occur more frequently in debates than other campaign media.

> H6. Defenses will be more common in debates than in other message forms.

Social media are built around people; Tweets and Facebook posts are very likely to be personal in nature. This could mean a different emphasis on topics compared with other media.

> H7. Social media will discuss character more, and policy less, than other media.

This does not necessarily mean that character will be the most common topic—although it could be—just that social media are likely to emphasize character more than other media. Notice that if it turns out that social media stress character more than policy, this would be an exception to H2.

Functional Theory anticipates that messages from the primary phase of the campaign will differ in predictable ways from general election messages. The primary phase pits candidates against other members of the same political party. In 2016, for example, Donald Trump contested the Republican nomination with Jeb Bush, Ben Carson, Chris Christie, Ted Cruz, Mike Huckabee, Ron Paul, Marco Rubio, and Scott Walter. Hillary Clinton ran against Lincoln Chafee, Martin O'Malley, Bernie Sanders, and Jim Webb. Of course, no two candidates are identical, even when they affiliate with the same political party (see the second assumption of Functional Theory). Still, greater differences are likely to exist when candidates of *different* parties clash in the general election than when members of the *same* party contest their party's nomination.

Another difference between primary and general elections is that generally candidates are less well-known in the primary than the general election. In 2016, for example, relatively few people knew Ben Carson and his issue positions. Donald Trump was a celebrity but little was known about his policy positions. The same can be said for other candidates such as John Kasich, Ted Cruz, Marco Rubio and Bernie Sanders. The candidates' need to introduce themselves in the primary is a reason to stress character in that phase.

> H8. Character should be more common, and policy less frequent, in the primary than the general campaign.

Fewer policy differences among candidates in the primaries means fewer opportunities to attack; more policy differences in the general campaign mean more opportunities to attack. Furthermore, candidates in the primary campaign phase have an incentive to moderate their attacks: Every candidate wants the losing opponents to support him or her in the general election. So for example, if Ted Cruz had won the 2016 Republican primary, he would have wanted Ben Carson, Marco Rubio, Chris Christie, John Kasich, and the others to advocate for him during the general campaign. Even more importantly, every nominee in the general election wants the support of all party members, including those who preferred a different candidate during the primary. Both of these considerations (support from other candidates, support from other candidates' partisans) provide a reason to moderate attacks in the primary, so as not to offend other candidates or the other candidates' supporters. This constraint does not exist in the general election campaign. For example, Benoit (2014a) isolated presidential candidates who won their party's nomination and who therefore deployed both primary TV spots and general ads: 21 of the 22 candidates acclaimed more, and attacked less, in their primary ads than they did in their general spots. Attacks do occur in the primary, but are likely less common that they are in the general election.

> H9. More attacks, and fewer acclaims, will be used in general election messages than in primary messages.

Furthermore, as noted earlier, fewer policy differences exist between members of the same party (in the primary) than between nominees from different political parties. It is easier for candidates to differentiate themselves from candidates of the other party than candidates of the same political party. Data comparing TV spots from primary and general campaigns confirm this prediction. When looking exclusively at presidential candidates who ran spots in both phases of the campaign, 20 of 22 candidates' ads were consistent with this prediction (Benoit, 2014a).

The next research question investigates similarities and differences between 2016 and previous presidential campaigns.

> RQ4. How do the data from the 2016 presidential campaign compare with data from previous elections?

Can we find consistency in trends over time?

The second research question concerns the relative frequency of the three forms of policy in these data.

> RQ5. Are there consistencies in the relative frequency of the three forms of policy?

The final research question addresses the relative frequency of the three forms of character in these data.

> RQ6. Are there consistencies in the relative frequency of the three forms of character?

The tests of these predictions and answers to these research questions will add to our understanding of political campaign messages.

Procedures

Functional Theory unitizes utterances into themes, which are complete ideas, claims, or arguments; a single theme can vary in length from a phrase to an entire paragraph (each of the examples in this chapter's appendix illustrate themes). The coders first identified themes present in the texts. Then each theme was categorized by function: acclaim, attack or defense. Third, coders categorized the topic of each theme as policy or character. Then coders identified the form of policy or character for each theme. Finally, the sponsor of each ad was identified. Benoit (2017) includes the codebook that guided this process.

Reliability

Cohen's κ was used for calculating inter-coder reliability because this statistic controls for agreement by chance. Reliability was calculated on about 10% of the debate texts. The κs for function were .91, for target of attack .84, for topic .87 for topic, .89 for forms of policy and .83 for forms of character. Reliability was also calculated on a sample of 10% of each of the two acceptance addresses, yielding the following *kappa*s: for classifying themes as acclaims, attacks, and defenses: .89; for classifying themes as policy or character: .78; for classifying policy themes as past deeds, future plans, or general goals: .91 for classifying character themes as personal qualities, leadership ability, or ideals: .86. Landis and Koch (1977) indicate that these levels of agreement are acceptable: κs of .81 and above reflect "almost perfect" agreement (p. 165). Examples of acclaims and attacks on the forms of policy and character are provided in Appendix 2.1.

Appendix 2.1: *Examples of Acclaims and Attacks on the Forms of Policy and Character*

Hillary Clinton's Primary Twitter Feed

Policy

Past Deeds

Acclaim: Madeleine Albright: "When she [Clinton] was Secretary of State, she repaired America's reputation around the world" (February 6, 2016)

Attack: "We need to face up to the reality of systemic racism" (February 18, 2016)

Future Plans

Acclaim: "$20 billion for programs to help young people get jobs and combat racial disparities in youth unemployment. $5 billion in programs to help formerly incarcerated people get jobs. $25 billion to support small businesses in under served communities. Paid for by a tax on Wall Street" (February 16, 2016)

Attack: "Hillary Clinton's Senior Foreign Policy Advisor, Jake Sullivan, responds to @BernieSanders' plans for ISIS and Iran [he criticizes three proposals from Sanders]" (January 21, 2016)

General Goals

Acclaim: Clinton supports "lifesaving cancer screenings, birth control, sex education" (February 17, 2016)

Attack: "There's only one thing standing between Republicans & repeal of the Affordable Care Act: a Democratic president" (January 28, 2016)

Character

Personal Qualities

Acclaim: "We need to recognize our privilege and practice humility" (February 16, 2016)

Attack: "Bluster and chest-beating aren't a strategy to defeat terrorism. #GOPdebate" (January 28, 2016)

Leadership Ability

Acclaim: "There are two candidates on stage at the #DemDebate. Only one is ready to be commander in chief" (February 11, 2016)

Attack: "Meet seven Republican candidates [in the primary debate] who are totally unprepared to be commander in chief" (January 28, 2016)

Ideals

Acclaim: "'Practice the discipline of gratitude.' Hillary on faith" (February 4, 2016)

Attack: "It wasn't very progressive [for Sanders] to vote against the Brady Bill five times, and immigration reform" (February 4, 2016)

Donald Trump's General Facebook Page

Policy

Past Deeds

Acclaim: "I am PROUD to have Mike Pence as my running mate. He balanced his budget and finished his term with $2 billion in the bank" (Donald Trump, October 4)

Attack: "It amazes me that people who live in the worst part of the country that Democrats have ruined, Detroit, Chicago still vote for HRC" (Clint Pierce, November 7)

Future Plans

Acclaim: "My childcare plan reflects the needs of modern day working-class families 100% deductible childcare expenses" (Donald Trump, September 30)

Attack: "#CrookedHillary has called for 550% more Syrian immigrants" (Donald Trump, October 19)

General Goals

Acclaim: I will "bring jobs and education to all the communities of Florida" (Donald Trump, November 7)

Attack: "Why are you [gays] voting for Hillary when she wants to bring in thousands of refugees that believe all Gays should be executed" (Johnathan Kibler, November 7)

Character

Personal Qualities

Acclaim: "Thank you [Donald Trump] for being BRAVE" (Leslie Houia Wright, November 7)

Attack: "They don't come any more corrupt than Hillary Clinton" (Godswill Forche, November 7)

Leadership Ability

Acclaim: "We need leaders like… Donald Trump" (Ajay Sharma, November 4)

Attack: "Hillary could not get her health care plan through the Senate when Bill was president" (Rose Anne Young-Bovee, October 25)

Ideals

Acclaim: "Conservatives believe in personal responsibility" (Anthony Cucuzza, November 4)

Attack: "Hillary will settle for nothing less than the total destruction of the American Dream" (Sue Davis, October 25)

General Presidential Debates

Policy

Past Deeds

Acclaim: "I voted for border security in the United States Senate" (Clinton, D3)
Attack: "We have 33,000 people a year who die from guns" (Clinton, D3)

Future Plans

Acclaim: "We need comprehensive background checks, need to close the online loophole, close the gun show loophole" (3 FP; Clinton, D3)
Attack: "What Donald is proposing with these massive tax cuts will result in a $20 trillion additional national debt" (Clinton, D3)

General Goals

Acclaim: "I want to build a wall" (Trump, D3)
Attack: "Hillary wants to give amnesty" to illegal immigrants (Trump, D3)

Character

Personal Qualities

Acclaim: "You can look at our tax returns. We've got them all out there" (Clinton, D3)
Attack: Clinton is "such a nasty woman" (Trump, D3)

Leadership Ability

Acclaim: "I was in the Situation Room, monitoring the raid that brought Osama bin Laden to justice" (Clinton, D3)
Attack: "This is a person who has been very cavalier, even casual about the use of nuclear weapons" (Clinton, D3)

Ideals

Acclaim: "I also believe there's an individual right to bear arms" (Clinton, D3)
Attack: Trump has said "women don't deserve equal pay unless they do as good a job as men" (Clinton, D1)

CHAPTER THREE

Candidacy Announcement Speeches

> I believe in you. I believe in the power of millions of courageous conservatives rising up to reignite the promise of America. And that is why today, I am announcing that I am running for President of the United States. (Ted Cruz, 3/23/15)

> Today, here in our small state—a state that has led the nation in so many ways—I am proud to announce my candidacy for president of the United States of America. Today, with your support and the support of millions of people throughout this country, we begin a political revolution to transform our country economically, politically, socially and environmentally. Today, we stand here and say loudly and clearly that; "Enough is enough. This great nation and its government belong to all of the people, and not to a handful of billionaires, their Super-PACs and their lobbyists." (Bernie Sanders, 5/26/15)

> This is our time to once again make our government a government of the people, by the people and for the people. That is why today I am declaring my candidacy for President. I will Make America Great Again! (Donald Trump, 6/16/15)

> Leadership means perseverance and hard choices. You have to push through the setbacks and disappointments and keep at it. I think you know by now that I've been called many things by many people—"quitter" is not one of them. (Hillary Clinton, 6/13/15)

Candidates for the Oval Office often visit key primary states in the months and years leading up to the election. They often form exploratory committees to begin collecting campaign donations and suss out how much support exists for their candidacy. Trent and Friedenberg (2004) characterize this period of time as the surfacing phase of the primary campaign. Sooner or later serious candidates make their candidacy formal by giving a candidacy announcement speech. It is not clear when the first presidential candidacy announcement speech occurred. Chen and Stracqualursi (2015) relate the fact that Abraham Lincoln gave a speech proclaiming his candidacy for president at the Illinois Republican State Convention in 1860.

The announcement address offers candidates a chance to introduce themselves to both voters and the news media as a candidate for the presidency, previewing the themes—policy and character—on which they intend to found their campaign. This is an important opportunity to create an initial impression of the candidate with voters that could influence the way in which he or she is perceived throughout of the campaign. It is possible to change initial impressions of a person, but "first impressions can have considerable effect on person perception" (Bromley, 1993, p. 36), so clearly it is better to start a presidential run with a favorable impression. The declaration of intent to run for president has been generally accepted as an important event in the modern campaign. Both voters and the news media expect to learn something about candidates in this speech. Finally, the announcement speech is an opportunity for candidates to attract media attention and coverage, so important at the beginning of a presidential campaign. In fact, during the 2000 campaign Dan Quayle appeared on Larry King Live to announce that he shortly would be giving an announcement speech! Announcing one's candidacy can serve a strategic function. It is possible than an early announcement may discourage other potential contenders from diving in. An announcement can also attract donations from supporters. Today it may seem as if the money available for campaigning is inexhaustible, but announced candidates may soak up most of the available donations, hindering other potential candidates.

Literature Review

Announcement speeches are a component of presidential candidates' pre-primary activities, called the surfacing phase (Trent, 1978, 1994, 1998). Trent and Friedenberg (2004) explained that seven functions are performed in the surfacing phase of a political campaign. First, announcement speeches proclaim a candidate's "fitness for office" (p. 25). Second, this phase constitutes the beginning of political campaign ritual. Third, this speech should convey the candidate's "goals, potential programs, or initial stands on issues" to voters and the news media (p. 28). Voters can learn about the candidate's personal style during surfacing, a fourth function of announcements. A fifth function is to identify the major themes of a presidential campaign. Sixth, the surfacing phase indicates which people are the serious contenders for the Oval Office. Finally, relationships develop between candidates and the news media in the surfacing phase. These ideas constitute several reasons for studying announcement speeches.

Of course, the surfacing phase consists of more than the announcement speech, but messages are arguably the most prominent component of this phase of presidential campaigns. Politicians who intend to run for president frequently visit early primary states, such as Iowa, New Hampshire, or South Carolina. They also often form "exploratory committees" to begin their campaign fund raising. However, the announcement speech is the official kick-off of one's candidacy for president.

The first Functional analysis on this message form investigated candidacy announcement speeches from 1960 to 2004 (Benoit et al., 2008). This study was supplemented by an analysis of announcements from 2008 to 2012 (Benoit & Glantz, 2013). Combining the data from these two studies, acclaims constituted 77% of themes, attacks were 23% of remarks, and defenses comprised 3% of statements. These speeches were more balanced in their use of the two topics: 52% policy and 48% character. Forms of policy were 36% past deeds, 11% future plans, and 53% general goals. General goals were employed more often to acclaim than to attack. When discussing character, these messages addressed personal qualities (33%), leadership ability (18%), and ideals (49%). Ideals were more often the basis for acclaims than attacks. These data provide a baseline for understanding the 2016 presidential announcement speeches.

Neville-Shepard (2014) offered three case studies of presidential third-party candidacy announcement speeches. He argues that speeches from these candidates are a distinct sub-genre of announcement speeches. Third-party candidates, in contemporary campaigns, have no realistic chance of reaching the Oval Office and suffer from several disadvantages: inadequate funding, exclusion from debates, and spotty coverage from the news media. As a result, these speeches acknowledge that victory cannot be expected so they attempt to disrupt the campaign so as to raise awareness of issues they champion, hoping to focus the major party candidates on these issues.

Sample

Texts were obtained from the Internet; the webpage 4President.org was especially helpful for finding texts. Announcements were obtained for three Democrats—Clinton, O'Malley, and Sanders—and 14 Republicans—Bush, Carson, Christie, Cruz, Jindal, Graham, Huckabee, Kasich, Pataki, Paul, Perry, Rubio, Trump, and

Walker. Appendix 3.1 lists their announcements organized by date. These texts were content analyzed with the same procedures employed in the two prior studies of announcements as well as in the other chapters in this book.

Results

Overall, the candidates in these announcement speeches from 2016 were mainly positive: 71% acclaims, 28% attacks, and only 0.2% defenses. Defenses clearly were the least frequent function in these speeches. Statistical analysis confirms Hypothesis 1, with acclaims significantly more common than attacks (χ^2 [df = 1] = 266.54, $p < .0001$). Table 3.1 shows that acclaims were the most common function in each candidate's announcement.

Table 3.1. Functions and Topics of 2016 Presidential Candidacy Announcement Speeches.

	Functions			Topics	
	Acclaims	Attacks	Defenses	Policy	Character
Clinton	127 (82%)	27 (18%)	0	86 (56%)	68 (44%)
O'Malley	59 (75%)	20 (25%)	0	57 (72%)	22 (28%)
Sanders	94 (54%)	80 (46%)	0	90 (71%)	37 (29%)
Democrats	**280 (69%)**	127 (31%)	0	**233 (65%)**	127 (35%)
Bush	63 (60%)	41 (39%)	1 (1%)	56 (54%)	48 (46%)
Carson	18 (75%)	6 (25%)	0	10 (42%)	14 (58%)
Christie	46 (72%)	18 (28%)	0	17 (27%)	47 (73%)
Cruz	57 (83%)	12 (17%)	0	32 (46%)	37 (54%)
Jindal	58 (63%)	34 (37%)	0	39 (42%)	53 (58%)
Graham	64 (75%)	21 (25%)	0	43 (51%)	42 (49%)
Huckabee	51 (52%)	48 (48%)	0	56 (57%)	43 (43%)
Kasich	64 (89%)	8 (11%)	0	28 (39%)	44 (61%)
Pataki	59 (77%)	16 (21%)	2 (3%)	35 (47%)	40 (53%)
Paul	63 (73%)	23 (27%)	0	48 (56%)	38 (44%)
Perry	57 (61%)	37 (39%)	0	48 (51%)	46 (49%)
Rubio	35 (67%)	17 (33%)	0	24 (46%)	28 (54%)
Trump	33 (54%)	28 (46%)	0	45 (74%)	16 (26%)
Walker	75 (82%)	17 (18%)	0	51 (55%)	41 (45%)
Republicans	**743 (69%)**	326 (30%)	3 (0.3%)	532 (50%)	537 (50%)
Total 2016	**1023 (69%)**	453 (31%)	3 (0.2%)	**765 (54%)**	664 (46%)

Total Acclaims vs. Attacks: χ^2 (df = 1) = 266.54, $p < .0001$
Total Topics 2016: χ^2 (df = 1) = 7.14, $p < .01$

For example, Sanders observed that "I've introduced legislation which would invest $1 trillion over five years to modernize our country's physical infrastructure. This legislation would create and maintain at least 13 million good-paying jobs" (5/26/15). These are goals that are likely to be perceived favorably by his audience. Trump decried the current situation: "Our country has a debt which will soon pass $20 trillion. We have unsecured borders. There are over 90 million Americans who have given up looking for work. We have 45 million Americans on food stamps and nearly 50 million Americans living in poverty" (6/16/15). These attacks should resonate with Republicans.

Examples of attacks can be found in announcement speeches as well. For instance, Clinton declared in her announcement speech that "Republicans trip over themselves promising lower taxes for the wealthy and fewer rules for the biggest corporations without regard for how that will make income inequality even worse" (6/13/15). These criticisms, attacking Republican goals of lower taxes for the wealthy and fewer rules for corporations, probably would be viewed as attacks by her target audience. Similarly, Bush criticized Democrats, asserting that "they are responsible for the slowest economic recovery ever, the biggest debt increases ever, a massive tax increase on the middle class, the relentless buildup of the regulatory state, and the swift, mindless drawdown of a military that was generations in the making." His audience is certain to view these statements as concerns.

Defenses were rare, but did occur in this sample of speeches. Some critics lamented the Bush "dynasty," with two presidents from this family (George Bush 41 and George W. Bush 43) serving a combined three terms in office. Jeb Bush's speech attempted to defuse this criticism: "And not a one of us deserves the job by right of resume, party, seniority, family, or family narrative" (6/15/15). This defense denied that he was entitled to the Oval Office because of his family.

The first research question concerned distribution of targets of attacks in Announcement Speeches. In this sample most attacks were aimed at the other party (91%; Democrats 100%, Republicans 89%). These data are displayed in Table 3.2.

Turning to the second hypothesis on topics of these texts, policy was somewhat more common than character 54% to 46%. However, the prominence of policy was consistent across the three Democrats in this sample, but 7 out of 13 Republicans stressed character over policy. These differences were statistically significant (χ^2 [df = 1] = 7.14, $p < .01$). These data are also displayed in Table 3.1. This finding should be considered conditional support for H2.

Next we will illustrate these two topics. Trump discussed several policy topics, including immigration:

> It is way past time to build a massive wall to secure our southern border—and nobody can build a bigger and better wall than Donald Trump. A country without borders is,

Table 3.2. Target of Attack in 2016 Presidential Announcement Speeches.

	Own Party	Other Party
Clinton		23
O'Malley		
Sanders		
Democrats		**23 (100%)**
Bush	2	28
Carson		
Christie		1
Cruz		8
Jindal	6	13
Graham	1	3
Huckabee	1	11
Kasich		
Pataki		3
Paul	1	3
Perry		10
Rubio	1	1
Trump		3
Walker		9
Republicans	12 (11%)	**93 (89%)**
Grand Total	12 (9%)	**121 (91%)**

Note. Attacks on the *status quo* (problems that need solutions) were omitted from this analysis.

> quite simply, not a country. Mexico is not our friend. They are beating us at the border and hurting us badly at economic development. They are sending people that they don't want—the United States is becoming a dumping ground for the world. (6/16/15)

This utterance is all about policy. Most of it happens to be an attack (the proposal for a border wall is an acclaim on general goals), but all of it is about policy.

> Rubio provides another example of a policy utterance: "If we reform our tax code, reduce regulations, control spending, modernize our immigration laws and repeal and replace ObamaCare, the American people will create millions of better-paying modern jobs" (4/13/15).

This utterance is an acclaim on policy that exemplifies several general goals.

Kasich offers an example of an utterance on character: "And I have to humbly tell you—and I mean humbly tell you—that I believe I do have the skills, and I have the experience" (July 24, 2015). Humility is considered a personal quality whereas his experience concerns leadership ability, both character traits (and, by the way, this statement is also an acclaim). Cruz proclaims that "It is a time for truth. It is a time for liberty. It is a time to reclaim the Constitution of the United States. I am honored to stand with each and every one of you. Courageous conservatives" (3/23/15). Honesty and courage are personal qualities whereas liberty and conservatism illustrate ideals (and all of these utterances are acclaims).

The first research question concerns the three forms of policy. In this sample, past deeds comprised 39% of policy utterances, future plans were 3% of policy themes, and most policy statements were general goals which constitute 58% of utterances. This distribution is statistically significant (χ^2 [*df* = 2]) = 370.52, $p <$ .0001). The third hypothesis, about functions of general goals, was also significant (χ^2 [*df* = 1]) = 317.52, $p <$ .0001). See Table 3.3 for these data.

RQ2 addresses the distribution of the three forms of character. When discussing character, these announcement speeches concerned personal qualities (36%), leadership ability (17%), and ideals (47%). These frequencies were significantly different (χ^2 [*df* = 2] = 30.44, $p <$ .0001). As H4 anticipated, ideals acclaimed more than they attacked (χ^2 [*df* = 1] = 144.41, $p <$ .0001). These data are displayed in Table 3.4.

Table 3.3. Forms of Policy in 2016 Presidential Candidacy Announcement Speeches.

	Past Deeds		Future Plans		General Goals	
	Acclaims	Attacks	Acclaims	Attacks	Acclaims	Attacks
Democrats	18	58	4	0	143	10
Republicans	49	180	14	2	271	26
2016 Total	67	238	18	2	414	36
	305 (39%)		20 (3%)		**450 (58%)**	

Form of Policy: χ^2 (*df* = 2) = 370.52, $p <$ .0001
Functions of General Goals: χ^2 (*df* = 1) = 317.52, $p <$ .0001

Table 3.4. Forms of Character in 2016 Presidential Candidacy Announcement Speeches.

	Personal Qualities		Leadership Ability		Ideals	
	Acclaims	Attacks	Acclaims	Attacks	Acclaims	Attacks
Democrats	45	6	16	2	24	3
Republicans	151	48	71	57	187	23
2016 Total	196	54	87	59	211	26
	250 (39%)		146 (23%)		237 (37%)	

Forms of Character: χ^2 (*df* = 2) = 30.44, $p <$ .0001
Functions of Ideals: χ^2 (*df* = 1) = 144.41, $p <$ .0001

Discussion and Conclusion

The data from 2016 are consistent with data on previous announcement speeches as well as with Functional Theory predictions. These speeches marked the "official" beginning of the presidential primary campaign. Acclaims, as predicted, were more common than attacks in both current and earlier speeches, as predicted. Defenses, also as predicted, were the least common functions. Functional Theory posits that candidates have reasons to stress acclaims, to avoid backlash against mudslinging. It also argues that defenses have three potential drawbacks (defending appears reactive more than proactive, a defense requires identifying a potential weakness, and defending is likely to take a candidate off-message) which makes defenses the least common function. Examination of Table 3.1 shows that the functions of announcement speeches in this sample clearly and consistently support this prediction.

The candidates in these speeches attacked the other party in quite a few comments (91%); they rarely attacked other members of their own party. Attacks are intended to reduce the favorability of the target. However, candidates are likely to benefit most from attacks on stronger opponents but at this early stage of the campaign (announcements) it is not easy to see who the strongest opponent will be. As Chapter 1 noted, Jeb Bush appeared to be far ahead of Donald Trump in the early primary season. Furthermore, at the beginning of the primary, candidates should be reluctant to alienate candidates who might endorse them later (and to alienate the target's supporters, who will shift their support when their preferred candidate drops out). By this reasoning, attacks on a candidate's own party members should be expected later in the campaign, rather than earlier.

More remarks addressed policy than character, although these topics were fairly evenly discussed in these speeches. Table 3.1 shows the distribution of topics is less consistent than the distribution of functions: All three Democratic candidates stressed policy more than character; half of the Republican candidates emphasized policy whereas half stressed character. Some evidence suggests that Democrats are prone to discuss policy more, and character less, than Republicans. Analysis of the data from 1960 to 2004 (Benoit et al., 2008) and from 2008 to 2012 (Benoit & Glantz, 2013) found that Democrats discussed policy more (56% to 45%) and character less (55% to 44%) than Republicans. This difference is significant (χ^2 [df = 1] = 53.01, p < .0001, φ = .1). Benoit (2004) suggested that Democrats are prone to propose governmental solutions to problems than Republicans, who are inclined to rely on private charity.

This could account for a differential emphasis on policy and character by political party. As anticipated, general goals and ideals were both used more often in service of acclaims than attacks. Functional Theory holds that it is easier to acclaim a goal or an ideal than to attack on these topics.

Appendix 3.1: *Dates of 2016 Presidential Candidacy Announcement Speeches*

Democratic

Bernie Sanders 5/26/15
Martin O'Malley 5/30/15
Hillary Clinton 6/13/15

Republican

Ted Cruz 3/23/15
Rand Paul 4/7/15
Marco Rubio 4/13/15
Ben Carson 5/4/15
Mike Huckabee 5/5/15
George Pataki 5/28/15
Lindsey Graham 6/1/15
Rick Perry 6/4/15
Jeb Bush 6/15/15
Donald Trump 6/16/15
Bobby Jindal 6/24/15
Chris Christie 6/30/15
Scott Walker 7/13/15
John Kasich 7/24/15

CHAPTER FOUR

Primary Television Spots

Announcer:	Think about it...
Donald Trump:	I would bomb the [bleep] out of them...
Announcer:	One of these Republicans...
Ted Cruz:	Carpet bomb them into oblivion...
Announcer:	Could actually be president...
Chris Christie:	Sit down and shut up...
Announcer:	Enacting their agenda...
Jeb Bush:	I think we should repeal Obamacare...
Donald Trump:	...our wages are too high...
Ted Cruz:	...defund Planned Parenthood...
Male Announcer:	They're backward, even dangerous. Who's the one candidate who can stop them? Hillary Clinton. Tested and tough. To stop them, stand with her. (Clinton, "Incredible," 2016)

From postal workers to nurses, he's been endorsed for real change. Bernie Sanders. Endorsed by Friends of the Earth Action as a bold, fearless voice for the planet. *The Nation* endorses Bernie, saying, you "can trust Bernie because he doesn't owe his political career to the financial overlords." The *Nashua Telegraph* declares "he's not beholden to Wall Street money." The *Valley News* says "Sanders has been genuinely outraged about the treatment of ordinary Americans for as long as we can remember." (Sanders, "Endorsed," 2016)

President Obama gave away the store to the Iranians—to a group of people who since 1979 have been chanting death to America. This was negotiated so badly that you wouldn't let this President buy a car for you at a car dealership. Now he's lying to the American people about how the deal's going to work. I would have walked away from the table. (Christie, "Protect America," 2016)

Announcer: Donald Trump's record? Support and defend Planned Parenthood. Government-funded healthcare. Let illegal aliens take our jobs. Who's looking out for us?

Cruz: The truck drivers and the steelworkers and the mechanics who've seen their wages not grow while the cost of living goes up. As President, I'll repeal Obamacare, I'll pull back the regulators. And we will pass a simple flat tax and abolish the IRS. We're going to see wages going up. We're going to see opportunity. (Cruz, "Looking Out," 2016)

Introduction

Presidential primary TV spots are important for a variety of reasons. First, no candidate in recent history has become president without first winning his or her political party's nomination. However, actually campaigning in primaries was not always necessary to secure the nomination. Richard Nixon won the presidential election in 1968 against Hubert Humphrey despite the fact that Humphrey did not campaign in the primaries (he was being loyal to President Lyndon Johnson, who was the likely Democratic nominee before he dropped out). Democrats, who loathed Nixon, changed the nomination process to make primary votes binding; Republicans made similar changes. From 1972 onward, candidates from both major political parties had to campaign (and win) in order to secure the parties' nominations. Third, some years feature a vulnerable nominee, such as Gerald Ford in 1976, Jimmy Carter in 1980, or George Bush in 1992. This may have meant that the crucial contest was the race for the nomination in the *other* political party, as candidates scrambled to win the right to face a relatively weak opponent.

Presidential candidates spent literally hundreds of millions of dollars on television advertising in the 2016 primary (although Trump spent less than recent nominees). Presidential candidates spent millions of dollars on television spots (in millions, through May 2016, "Estimated cost of ads," 2016):

Bernie Sanders	$73.7
Marco Rubio	$72.7
Jeb Bush	$66.9
Hillary Clinton	$62.6
Ted Cruz	$37.6
John Kasich	$18.9
Donald Trump	$18.5

Chris Christie	$14.6
Ben Carson	$4.3
Bobby Jindal	$3.8
Rand Paul	$1.7
Lindsey Graham	$1.4
Rick Perry	$1.1
Mike Huckabee	$1
Carly Fiorina	$0.5

In total, these candidates spent $379.3 million on primary advertising. This money paid for over 250 ads, with individual ads airing many times. These messages had the opportunity to influence primary voters.

Finally, research has firmly established that both TV spots and debates have important effects on viewers in the primary (see, e.g., Benoit, Leshner, & Chattopadhyay, 2007; Benoit, Hansen, & Verser, 2003). Ads have been found to increase knowledge of the issues in a campaign, affect the perceived importance of issues (agenda-setting), alter perceptions of candidates' character, change attitudes toward the candidates, affect candidate preference, and change the likelihood that viewers would vote in the election. Other messages forms surely have effects as well; however the evidence for effects of TV spots (and debates) is particularly strong.

Literature Review

Presidential candidate TV spots have been a part of primary campaigns as early as 1952, which was the first presidential campaign to use this medium (Benoit, 2014a). As predicted by Functional Theory, presidential candidates used acclaims (72%) more than attacks (28%), and attacks more than defenses (1%), in primary contests (Benoit, 2014a). These messages showed a slight emphasis on policy (54% policy, 46% character). Presidential primary candidates acclaimed more than they attacked when discussing general goals and ideals (Benoit, 2014a). A review of specific studies on presidential primary TV spots can be found in Benoit (2014a). Benoit and Glantz (2017) offer an in-depth investigation of attacks in 2016 Republican primary television advertisements.

Sample

This study of 2016 presidential primary TV spots includes candidates for both the Democratic and Republican nomination. Two Democrats were included: Clinton (60 ads) and Sanders (45 ads). The Republicans in this sample were Bush (11 ads), Carson (13 ads), Christie (9 ads), Cruz (44 ads), Fiorina (3 ads), Gilmore (1 ad), Graham (3 ads), Huckabee (1 ad), Kasich (12 ads), Paul (7 ads), Perry (1 ad), Rubio (29 ads), Santorum (2 ads), Trump (12 ads), and Walker (1 ad). The total number of candidate spots in the sample was 257. We also located 171 group sponsored TV spots.

Results

The first prediction held that acclaims would be more common than attacks and defenses would be the least common function. This hypothesis was

Table 4.1. Functions and Topics of 2016 Presidential Primary TV Spots.

	Functions			Topics	
	Acclaims	Attacks	Defenses	Policy	Character
Clinton	**290 (76%)**	92 (24%)	0	**280 (83%)**	57 (17%)
Sanders	**133 (75%)**	45 (25%)	0	**116 (65%)**	62 (35%)
Democratic	**423 (82%)**	92 (18%)	0	**396 (77%)**	119 (23%)
Bush	**74 (85%)**	13 (15%)	0	**45 (52%)**	42 (48%)
Carson	**16 (55%)**	13 (45%)	0	11 (38%)	**18 (62%)**
Christie	**13 (54%)**	11 (46%)	0	**14 (58%)**	10 (42%)
Cruz	**199 (68%)**	92 (31%)	3 (1%)	**166 (57%)**	125 (43%)
Fiorina	**12 (75%)**	4 (25%)	0	3 (19%)	**13 (81%)**
Gilmore	**4 (57%)**	3 (43%)	0	3 (43%)	**4 (57%)**
Graham	**23 (100%)**	0	0	3 (13%)	**20 (87%)**
Huckabee	**4 (80%)**	1 (20%)	0	2 (40%)	**3 (60%)**
Kasich	**46 (88%)**	6 (12%)	0	**27 (52%)**	25 (48%)
Paul	**22 (69%)**	10 (31%)	0	**17 (53%)**	15 (47%)
Perry	**4 (67%)**	2 (33%)	0	2 (33%)	**4 (67%)**
Rubio	**129 (84%)**	25 (16%)	0	60 (39%)	**94 (61%)**
Santorum	**7 (78%)**	2 (22%)	0	4 (44%)	**5 (55%)**
Trump	**26 (58%)**	19 (42%)	0	**28 (62%)**	17 (38%)
Walker	**14 (88%)**	2 (12%)	0	6 (37%)	**10 (63%)**
Republican	**593 (74%)**	203 (25%)	3 (0.4%)	391 (49%)	**405 (51%)**
2016 Total	**1016 (77%)**	295 (22%)	4 (0.3%)	**787 (60%)**	524 (40%)
Groups	**586 (66%)**	299 (34%)	5 (0.5%)	325 (37%)	**558 (63%)**

Acclaims vs. Attacks: χ^2 (df = 2) = 395.52, p < .0001
Topics: χ^2 (df = 1) = 52.76, p < .0001
Acclaims vs. Attacks for Candidates vs. Groups: χ^2 (df = 1) = 34.09, p < .0001, φ = .12

confirmed: acclaims were 77%, attacks 23%, and defenses were 0.3%. Defenses were obviously the least common function; a significant difference occurred between the frequency of acclaims and attacks (χ^2 [df = 2] = 395.52, p < .0001). Table 4.1 for these data shows that every candidate in this sample conformed to this prediction.

Kasich offered an acclaim in his spot "Progress" (2016): "As governor, Kasich delivered the largest tax cut in the nation and over 400,000 new jobs have been created through his leadership. As President, Kasich will cut taxes, freeze new regulations and restore American jobs." This statement touts his accomplishments as governor of Ohio, speaks with pride of his leadership ability, and proposes three general goals. All of these themes should be viewed positively by his audience. Democrat Sanders ("Two Visions," 2016) also used acclaims: "My plan: break up the big banks, close the tax loopholes, and make them pay their fair share. Then we can expand health care to all and provide universal college education." These five goals (break up banks, close loopholes, pay a fair share, health care for all, and a college education for all) would surely see these as desirable.

These spots also included attacks. For example, Republican Trump ran an ad attacking fellow Republican Cruz:

> When Marco Rubio became Speaker of the House, he brought his friends along for the ride. His spiritual advisor, Raf Arza, resigned from office after lobbing racial slurs and being convicted of witness tampering. His best friend and roommate, David Rivera, was found guilty of ethics violations and is currently under FBI investigation. Where are these friends today? Spotted on the campaign trail with Marco. ("Keep Marco and His Friends Out of the White House," 2016)

This ad uses guilt by association to denigrate Cruz. Clinton criticized business magnate Trump ("Stronger Together," 2016):

Announcer:	"He says we should punish women who have abortions."
Announcer:	"Donald Trump: There has to be some form of punishment."
Male Announcer:	"That Mexicans who come to America are rapists."
Donald Trump:	"They're rapists."
Male Announcer:	"And that we should ban Muslims from coming here at all."
Donald Trump:	"Total and complete shutdown."
Hillary Clinton:	"Donald Trump says we can solve America's problems by turning against each other. It's wrong, and it goes against everything New York and America stand for."

The attack uses Trump's own words to support Clinton's indictment of her likely general election opponent.

GOP member Cruz illustrated a defense when he said "Donald Trump is lying about Ted Cruz. Cruz voted against TPA and is fighting to stop TPP" ("Trump Lying About Ted Cruz," 2016). This statement identifies an attack (that Cruz supports the international trade agreements), a defense using denial ("Cruz voted against the TPA") and an acclaim on general goals (Cruz "is fighting to stop TPP").

The first research investigated which party received the most attacks in the primary. Combined, 61% of criticisms were aimed at the other party and 39% at other members of one's own party. However, Table 4.2 shows these data.

H2 predicted that policy would be more common than character in these texts. Policy constituted 54% whereas character comprised 46% of themes in these spots, confirming this prediction. This difference was significant (χ^2 [*df* = 1] = 52.76,

Table 4.2. Target of Attacks in 2016 Presidential Primary TV Spots.

	Bush	Carson	Christie	Cruz	Fiorina	Gilmore	Graham	Huckabee	Kasich	Paul	Perry	Rubio	Santorum	Trump	Walker	Repub	Status Quo	Demo	Clinton	Sanders
Clinton																30	38			1
Sanders																2	38			
Democrat																32	76		0	1
Bush												1		2		1	2	4		
Carson																1	2	3		
Christie												1					1	12		
Cruz	1	1							1			14		20		2	24	14		
Fiorina																		1		
Gilmore																		2		
Graham														1						
Huckabee																				
Kasich	4			1													3	2		
Paul																	4	5		
Perry																				
Rubio	2																9	16		
Santorum				1																
Trump				5					4			4					1			
Walker																				
Republican	7	1		7					5			20		23		4	86	68		
Total	7	1		7					5			20		23		36	162	68		1
									Own Party: 64 (39%)							Other Party: 100 (61%)				

$p < .0001$). Both Democratic candidates conformed to this prediction. However, we note that nine Republicans discussed character more than policy. These data are also displayed in Table 4.1.

Examples of the two topics of campaign discourse also abound in these texts. For instance, Clinton's ad "Came Through" addressed policy: "China. India. Some of the world's worst polluters. As Secretary of State, Hillary Clinton forced them to the table, making real change by laying the groundwork for the historical global agreement to combat climate change. As president, she'll invest in a clean energy future and the jobs that go with it, and stand firm with New Yorkers opposing fracking, giving communities the right to say no" (2016). These policy utterances acclaim her accomplishments as Secretary of State and acclaim her general goals. Her primary opponent also addressed policy concerns in his TV spots: "The NAFTA trade treaty. 850,000 jobs lost. Special trade status with China. 3 million jobs lost. Now the Trans-Pacific trade deal could cost America 448,000 more jobs" (Sanders, "Stood with American Workers," 2016). Foreign trade is a clear illustration of policy discussion.

Sanders ("Iowa Endorsements," 2016) also acclaimed his character in this ad:

> Bernie Sanders. Endorsed by Friends of the Earth Action as a bold, fearless voice for the planet. *The Nation* endorses Bernie, saying you "can trust Sanders because he doesn't owe his political career to the financial overlords." The *Des Moines Register* called him "a man of courage and principle."

Trust, courage, and principle are all instances of character discussion. Fellow-Democrat Clinton touted her perseverance, another character trait: ("Stood Strong, 2016"): "I've never been called a quitter and I won't quit on you." These excerpts illustrate how the candidates addressed both policy and character in their primary TV spots.

The first research question inquired about the relative proportion of the three forms of policy. In this sample, general goals were 42%, future plans were 6%, and general goals were 52% of policy utterances. This distribution was statistically significant (χ^2 [$df = 2$] = 271.82, $p < .0001$). Prediction H3 expected that general goals would be used more often to acclaim than to attack. This contrast was significant (χ^2 [$df = 1$] = 247.06, $p < .0001$). See Table 4.3.

RQ2 investigated the relative proportion of the three forms of character. These candidates devoted 52% to personal qualities, 12% leadership ability, and 30% to ideals. This distribution was significant (χ^2 [$df = 2$] = 98.72, $p < .0001$). Hypothesis four anticipated that ideals would form the basis for acclaims than attacks. This prediction was confirmed (χ^2 [$df = 1$] = 121.3, $p < .0001$). These data are reported in Table 4.4.

Table 4.3. Forms of Policy in 2016 Presidential Primary TV Spots.

	Past Deeds		Future Plans		General Goals	
2016 Democratic	124	54	19	2	173	24
	178 (45%)		21 (5%)		197 (50%)	
2016 Republican	80	72	7	21	187	24
	152 (39%)		28 (7%)		211 (54%)	
2016 Total	204	126	26	23	360	48
	330 (42%)		49 (6%)		408 (52%)	

Forms of Policy: χ^2 (df = 2) = 271.82, $p < .0001$
Functions of General Goals: χ^2 (df = 1) = 237.05, $p < .0001$

Table 4.4. Forms of Character in 2016 Presidential Primary TV Spots.

	Personal Qualities		Leadership Ability		Ideals	
2016 Democratic	57	11	26	0	24	1
	68 (57%)		26 (22%)		25 (21%)	
2016 Republican	142	66	53	12	124	8
	208 (51%)		65 (16%)		132 (33%)	
2016 Total	197	77	79	12	148	9
	274 (52%)		91 (17%)		157 (30%)	

Forms of Character: χ^2 (df = 2) = 98.72, $p < .0001$
Functions of Ideals: χ^2 (df = 1) = 121.3, $p < .0001$

The fifth hypothesis predicted that non-candidate sponsored TV spots would attack more, and acclaim less, than ads sponsored by candidates. Candidate ads acclaimed more (77% to 66%) and attacked less (22% to 34%) than spots from groups. Statistical analysis confirms that these differences are significant (χ^2 [df = 1] = 34.09, $p < .0001$, φ = .12). In this sample, both groups acclaimed more than they attacked; however, spots from groups acclaimed less, and attacked more, than candidate ads.

Discussion and Conclusion

This sample, and each candidate in it, acclaimed more frequently than they attacked. This is consistent with Functional Theory. Attacks have a drawback (potential backlash from those who dislike mudslinging) not shared by acclaims. Only one candidate used defense in political advertising. Functional Theory expects that defenses will be the least common function because it possesses three potential drawbacks (defenses usually take a candidate off-message, defenses must identify the attack they attempt to refute, which could inform or remind viewers of a possible weakness, and defenses could be perceived by voters as reactive rather than proactive).

Although these candidates attacked their own party and the opposing party. However, candidates from the opposing party absorbed the brunt of these attacks. Stressing opponents in attacks could have occurred because many of these spots were broadcast early in the campaign, when candidates should avoid offending the other candidates (who might offer an endorsement when they drop out) and the party voters who preferred that candidate.

As a group, these candidates talked more about policy than character. Both Democratic candidates emphasized policy. However, 9 out of 15 Republicans discussed character more than policy. Functional Theory anticipates that candidates will focus on policy more than character. Research (Benoit, 2004) found that in primary advertising, Republicans tend to discuss character more, and policy less, than Democrats. This could be because the GOP tends to prefer private solutions (e.g., charity) to problems more than governmental answers, so Democrats may stress policy more than Republicans.

The next two predictions were clearly upheld. In this sample candidates used general goals and ideals more as the basis of acclaims than attacks. Functional Theory argues that it is much easier to acclaim a goal (e.g., creating jobs) or an ideal (liberty) than to attack them.

Hypothesis 5, on source of spot, was also confirmed. Both candidate spots and group ads used more acclaims than attacks, as predicted by H1. However, candidates attacked in 22% of their primary TV spots whereas group sponsored advertisements attacked in 34% of statements. The idea here is that one can expect some backlash from attacks and it is better if most of the backlash impinges on groups than on candidates. It is not clear whether putting most attacks into the "mouths" of outside groups actually helps protect the candidates avoid backlash, but the data clearly support the prediction that sponsor of ad influences the content of ads.

CHAPTER FIVE

Primary Debates

In Florida… I cut taxes every year, totaling $19 billion. We balanced every budget. We went from $1 billion of reserves to $9 billion of reserves. We were one of two states that went to AAA bond rating. They called me Veto Corleone. Because I vetoed 2,500 separate line-items in the budget. I am my own man. I governed as a conservative, and I govern effectively. And the net effect was, during my eight years, 1.3 million jobs were created. (Bush, Republican Debate 1, 2015)

Our leaders are stupid. Our politicians are stupid. And the Mexican government is much smarter, much sharper, much more cunning. And they send the bad ones over because they don't want to pay for them. They don't want to take care of them. Why should they when the stupid leaders of the United States will do it for them? And that's what is happening whether you like it or not. (Trump, Republican Debate 1, 2015)

A majority of the candidates on this stage have supported amnesty. I have never supported amnesty, and I led the fight against Chuck Schumer's gang of eight amnesty legislation in the Senate. (Cruz, Republican Debate 1, 2015)

Let's start off with my father being a mailman. So I understand the concerns of all the folks across this country, some of whom having trouble, you know, making ends meet. (Kasich, Republican Debate 1, 2015)

You're living in a world of the make-believe, Chris [Christie]. (Trump, Republican Debate 1, 2015)

> I still remember, as a kid, tying a yellow ribbon around a tree in front of my house during the 444 days that Iran held 52 Americans hostage. (Walker, Republican Debate 1, 2015)

The president of the United States is the most powerful politician in the world. For decades, only candidates of the Democratic and Republican Parties has been elected president. This situation confers great importance on the primary race for the nomination. Unlike 2012, both political parties had contested presidential primaries in 2016. Both political parties saw presidential primary debates.

Presidential primary debates have been employed to help voters in America make a choice about who should be their party's nominee since 1948, when Dewey and Stassen participated in a debate on radio during the Oregon Republican primary campaign. In recent years primary debates have been much more common than debates in the general election campaign. In 2004, for instance, there were 21 primary, 3 presidential, and 1 vice presidential debates in the campaign (Benoit et al., 2007). In 2008 20 Democratic and 16 Republican primary debates were held (Benoit, Henson, & Sudbrock, 2011). The Democratic nomination was not contested in 2012; the Republican Party held 19 primary debates that year. In 2016 12 Republican primary debates were held (11 with Trump) and 9 Democratic primary debates (see Appendix 5.1). Various studies have found that voters can be influenced by presidential primary debates (see Benoit, 2014c for a review of specific studies). Meta-analysis has established that watching televised presidential primary debates can increase issue knowledge, affect perceptions of candidate character, and change vote choice (Benoit et al., 2003); these effects are even larger in primary than general debates, probably because voters have less knowledge, fewer character perceptions, and weaker commitment to vote choice early in the campaign. Balz (2012) argued that the Republican primary debates of 2012 made a difference: The debates "certainly mattered during the Republican nomination contest in the winter. Those 20 debates shaped the campaign and the fortunes of many of the candidates. Think Rick Perry." There is no question that presidential primary debates merit scholarly attention.

Although the average viewership for primary debates is less than for general election debates, many voters do watch primary debates. For example, in 2008, 24 of the Democratic and Republican primary debates attracted 90 million viewers (Kurtz, 2008; Memmott & Carnia, 2007; Page, 2008). Stelter (2016) observed that "Fox's GOP debate was watched by 24 million viewers on Thursday night." He added that "prime time GOP debate ratings this year are three to four time higher than they were in 2011." This audience was unusually large:

> The audience easily exceeded pretty much everything that's been on American television this year, from the finale of "The Walking Dead" to the final episode of

> David Letterman's "Late Show." The debate was bigger than all of this year's NBA Finals and MLB World Series games, and most of the year's NFL match-ups. It also trumped Jon Stewart's Thursday night's sign-off from "The Daily Show," which averaged 3.5 million viewers.

Furthermore, Nielson (2016) reported that "Overall, the first 12 debates—six each for both the Republican and Democratic events—reached 97 million Americans, with about equal numbers watching the Democratic debates (68 million) as those that watched the Republican debates (67 million)." These large audiences translate into an impressive opportunity to reach voters.

Literature Review

Compared with general election debates, relatively few studies have content analyzed American presidential primary debates. Benoit (2014c) offers a review of specific studies in this area. Benoit and Glantz (2017) dive deeply into the Republican primary debates in 2016. A study of American presidential primary debates from 1948 to 2000 offers some insights into the content of these messages (Benoit et al., 2002). Acclaims were the most common function of these primary debates (63%), followed by attacks (32%) and defenses (4%). When they did attack in primary debates, presidential candidates were more likely to attack members of their own political party (47%) than candidates in the opposing party (30%) or to attack the status quo (criticisms that indicted both major parties, 24%). More of these policy utterances concerned general goals (ends; 40%) or past deeds (record in office, 37%) than future plans (means, 24%). When the candidates discussed character in primary debates, they discussed ideals (45%) and personal qualities (36%) more than leadership ability (19%). Benoit et al. (2007) reported similar patterns: The Democratic primary debates of 2004 employed acclaims (63%) more than attacks (32%) or defenses (4%). One contrasting finding was that these Democratic candidates were more likely to direct attacks toward Republican President Bush (65%) than to one another (21%) or the establishment generally (15%). Benoit, Henson, and Sudbrook (2011) analyzed presidential primary debates in the 2008 election. Acclaims were again the most common function (68%), followed by attacks (26%) and defenses (6%). This pattern occurred in the 2012 primaries: 67% acclaims, 30% attacks, and 3% defenses (Glantz, Benoit, & Airne, 2013). A clear pattern emerges here, as predicted by Functional Theory: acclaims are the most common function of presidential primary debates, followed by attacks and then defenses.

The candidates in the primary debates from 1948 to 2000 discussed policy (63%) more frequently than character (37%; Glantz, Benoit, & Airne, 2012). About three-fourths of the candidates' themes in the 2004 primary debates concerned policy and the remainder character (Benoit et al., 2007). The candidates in 2008 discussed policy more than character (70% to 30%; Benoit, Henson, & Sudbrook, 2011). In 2012, presidential primary candidates discussed policy in about two-thirds of their comments (67%) and character in the remaining utterances (33%). Here again the pattern conforms to predictions from Functional Theory. We extend this line of analysis, deploying Functional Theory to analyze Democratic and Republican primary debates in the 2016 American presidential campaign.

Sample

This study reports content analyses of 11 Republican presidential primary debates (given his centrality to the campaign, the one Republican debate skipped by Trump was excluded from the sample) and 9 Democratic primary debates from the 2016 campaign. The candidates who participated in at least one of the Republican debates were Bush, Carson, Christie, Cruz, Fiorina, Huckabee, Kasich, Paul, Rubio, Trump, and Walker. The candidates appearing in the Democratic debates were: Chafee, Clinton, O'Malley, Sanders, and Webb. The appendix lists the debates included in this sample and participants in each one.

Results

This section presents the results of the content analysis of texts of the 2016 presidential primary debates. The first hypothesis concerned the functions of these presidential primary debates. As Table 5.1 indicates, acclaims (58%) occurred more frequently than attacks (34%), which in turn were employed more often than defenses (7%). These differences were statistically significant (χ^2 [df = 1] = 564.49, $p < .0001$). Clinton provided an example of an acclaim (all of the examples offered in this section were used in the second Democratic primary debate) when she declared that "we have to… go after the gun lobby and 92 percent of Americans agree we should have universal background checks. Close the gun show loophole, close the online loophole and I will do everything I can as president to get that accomplished." These proposals (go after the gun lobby, implement universal background checks, close the gun show loophole and close the online loophole are all acclaims). O'Malley acclaimed his past record in office: "Not only were we the first state in the nation to pass a living wage. We were the first to pass a minimum wage." Minimum wage accomplishments could appeal to many in the audience. Sanders

Table 5.1. Functions and Topics of 2016 Presidential Primary Debates.

	Functions			Topics	
	Acclaims	Attacks	Defenses	Policy	Character
Chafee	**52 (88%)**	4 (7%)	3 (5%)	**52 (93%)**	4 (7%)
Clinton	**818 (67%)**	282 (23%)	126 (10%)	**818 (74%)**	282 (26%)
O'Malley	**307 (72%)**	108 (25%)	11 (3%)	**307 (74%)**	108 (26%)
Sanders	**591 (53%)**	426 (38%)	102 (9%)	**591 (58%)**	426 (42%)
Webb	**44 (77%)**	10 (18%)	3 (5%)	**44 (81%)**	10 (19%)
Democratic	**1812 (63%)**	830 (29%)	248 (9%)	**1812 (68%)**	839 (32%)
Bush	**364 (60%)**	218 (36%)	23 (4%)	**383 (66%)**	199 (34%)
Carson	**209 (59%)**	121 (34%)	25 (7%)	**168 (56%)**	133 (44%)
Christie	**244 (53%)**	198 (43%)	20 (4%)	**270 (61%)**	172 (39%)
Cruz	**487 (52%)**	418 (44%)	40 (4%)	**560 (67%)**	271 (33%)
Fiorina	**140 (58%)**	89 (37%)	14 (6%)	**115 (62%)**	69 (38%)
Huckabee	**57 (66%)**	29 (33%)	1 (1%)	**60 (76%)**	19 (24%)
Kasich	**631 (79%)**	150 (19%)	20 (2%)	**578 (74%)**	203 (26%)
Paul	**117 (48%)**	118 (48%)	9 (4%)	**168 (71%)**	67 (29%)
Rubio	**392 (46%)**	406 (48%)	55 (6%)	**468 (61%)**	305 (39%)
Trump	**765 (56%)**	384 (28%)	210 (15%)	**791 (63%)**	457 (37%)
Walker	**64 (58%)**	46 (42%)	0	**35 (63%)**	21 (37%)
Republican	**3470 (56%)**	2276 (37%)	417 (7%)	**3596 (65%)**	1916 (35%)
2016 Total	**5282 (58%)**	3106 (34%)	665 (7%)	**5518 (68%)**	2636 (32%)

Acclaims vs. Attacks: χ^2 (df = 1) = 564.49, $p < .0001$
Topics: χ^2 (df = 1) = 1017.92, $p < .0001$

attacked the *status quo*, lamenting the fact that "People are working longer hours for lower wages, and almost all of the new income and wealth goes to the top one percent." This statement identifies problems that need to be fixed, presumably by Sanders. Clinton offered an attack on her opponent, Sanders. He "does eliminate the Affordable Care Act, eliminates private insurance, eliminates Medicare, eliminates Medicaid, Tricare, children's health insurance program eliminates private insurance, eliminates Medicare, eliminates Medicaid, Tricare, children's health insurance program." These changes are unlikely to be favored by many Democrats. Sanders presented a defense to one of these charges, declaring that "We don't eliminate Medicare." If accepted, this denial should deal with (part of) Clinton's criticism. Accused of raising taxes as Governor, O'Malley minimized the increase and offered a justification: "we did in fact raise the sales tax by a penny and we made our public schools the best public schools in America for five years in a row with that investment." So, these candidates made use of acclaims (most commonly), attacks, and defenses (least frequent). These data are reported in Table 5.1.

These data also address the question of target of attack. In these debates both groups of candidates criticized their own party more than they attacked the opposition party: Democrats 62% to 28%; Republicans 59% to 41%. Combined more attacks were directed toward a candidate's own party (60%) than the opposition (40%). These data are reported in Table 5.2.

Hypothesis two concerned the candidates' use of topics of discourse. The data show that policy (68%) was employed more frequently than character (32%). This contrast was statistically significant (χ^2 [df = 1] = 1017.92, $p < .0001$). To illustrate these data, Clinton addressed policy in this statement "We have a lot of work to do to get jobs going again, get incomes rising again." This utterance includes two themes, both acclaims, on jobs and income. Another example of a policy utterance comes from Sanders: "That billionaires pay an effective tax rate lower than nurses or truck drivers. That makes no sense at all. There has to be real tax reform, and

Table 5.2. Target of Attack in 2016 Presidential Primary Debates.

	Own Party	Other Party
Chafee	12	0
Clinton	131	63
O'Malley	41	60
Sanders	90	46
Web	2	1
Democrats	**276 (62%)**	170 (38%)
Bush	85	77
Carson	17	33
Christie	82	72
Cruz	190	157
Fiorina	19	21
Huckabee	2	10
Kasich	65	28
Paul	71	12
Rubio	161	137
Trump	200	58
Walker	6	21
Republicans	**898 (59%)**	626 (41%)
Total	**1174 (60%)**	796 (40%)

the wealthiest and large corporations will pay when I'm president." The first two statements are one attack and the third sentence is an acclaim, both on the policy of taxation. O'Malley gave this example of an acclaim on character (leadership ability): "There's a big difference between leading by polls and leading with principle. We got it done in my state by leading with principal." Another instance of a character utterance was O'Malley's criticism of Trump's personal qualities: Donald Trump is just "a carnival barker." These data are also displayed in Table 5.1.

The first RQ concerns the relative proportion of the three forms of policy. In the 2016 presidential primary debates the most common form of policy was general goals (56%). The next frequent kind of policy utterance was past deeds (35%). Future plans were the least common form of policy (8%). H3 anticipated that general goals were be used more often to acclaim than to attack. This prediction was confirmed in these data (acclaims were 87% whereas attacks were 13%). This contrast was statistically significant (χ^2 [df = 1] = 1916.05, p < .0001). These results can be found in Table 5.3.

Table 5.3. Forms of Policy in 2016 Presidential Primary Debates.

	Past Deeds		Future Plans		General Goals	
2016 Democratic	211	489	145	42	960	75
	700 (36%)		187 (10%)		1035 (54%)	
2016 Republican	329	920	212	69	1759	328
	1249 (33%)		381 (10%)		2087 (56%)	
2016 Total	540	1409	357	111	2719	403
	1949 (35%)		468 (8%)		3122 (56%)	

Forms of Policy: χ^2 (df = 2) = 1916.05, p < .0001
Functions of General Goals: χ^2 (df = 1) = 1718.08, p < .0001

Table 5.4. Forms of Character in 2016 Presidential Primary Debates.

	Personal Qualities		Leadership Ability		Ideals	
2016 Democratic	225	182	145	30	126	12
	407 (57%)		175 (24%)		138 (19%)	
2016 Republican	447	641	342	230	261	88
	1108 (55%)		572 (28%)		349 (17%)	
2016 Total	672	823	487	260	387	100
	1495 (55%)		747 (27%)		487 (18%)	

Forms of Character: χ^2 (df = 2) = 602.11, p < .0001
Functions of Ideals: χ^2 (df = 1) = 473.98 p < .0001

The third research question investigated the allocation of the three forms of character in these data. When addressing character, these candidates most frequently discussed personal qualities (55%), followed by leadership ability (27%), and then ideals (18%). The final hypothesis held that when the candidates used ideals they were more likely to acclaim than attack. Acclaims constituted 79% of ideals; attacks comprised 21% of ideals. This difference was statistically significant (χ^2 [$df = 1$] = 602.11 $p < .0001$). See Table 5.4 for these data.

Discussion and Conclusion

These data support the predictions of Functional Theory (Benoit, 2007) and conform to past research on past presidential primary debates (Benoit, 2014c). Acclaims were more common than attacks, which were used more often than defenses. Functional Theory explains that acclaims (although not necessarily persuasive) have no drawbacks. Attacks risk a potential backlash against mudslinging. Defenses have three potential drawbacks. A defense is likely to move a candidate off-message. Defenses may create the impression that a candidate using them is reactive rather than proactive. The third drawback, the risk of informing or reminding voters of a possible weakness, does not apply to debates because viewers see attacks before candidates respond to them. Although debates are the least common function, it should come as no surprise that defenses are more common in debates than other primary messages.

In the debates candidates attacked both political parties, but the emphasis shifted to a predominance of attacks against other members of one's own party. Unlike Announcement Speeches and TV spots, debates are more spontaneous. Candidates clearly prepare for debates, but candidates are not allowed notes, so debates have no script, unlike Announcements and TV spots. It may be difficult to resist the impulse to attack when a candidate is confronted by candidates in a live debate.

Candidates in these primary debates addressed policy more than character. This is consistent with Functional Theory and past work on the functions of primary debates (Benoit, 2014c). Both general goals and ideals were used more frequently as the basis of acclaims than attacks. Again, these findings are predicted by Functional Theory and confirmed by research on the topics of past presidential primary debates. This study extends our knowledge of this important message form; it also offers providing insights into the most recent election. This study adds to our knowledge of this important message form as well as providing insights into the most recent election.

Appendix 5.1: *Participation in 2016 Presidential Primary Debates*

Republican Primary Debates

1 Cleveland, OH August 6, 2015 Bush, Carson, Christie, Cruz, Huckabee, Kasich, Paul, Rubio, Trump, Walker
2 Simi Valley, CA 9/16/15 Bush, Carson, Christie, Cruz, Fiorina, Huckabee, Kasich, Paul, Rubio, Trump, Walker
3 Boulder, CO 10/28/15 Bush, Carson, Christie, Cruz, Fiorina, Huckabee, Kasich, Paul, Rubio, Trump
4 Milwaukee, WI 11/10/15 Bush, Carson, Cruz, Fiorina, Kasich, Paul, Rubio, Trump
5 Las Vegas, NV 12/15/15 Bush, Carson, Christie, Cruz, Fiorina, Kasich, Paul, Rubio, Trump
6 North Charleston, NC 1/14/16 Bush, Carson, Christie, Cruz, Kasich, Paul, Rubio, Trump
7 Des Moines, IA 1/28/16 Bush, Carson, Christie, Cruz, Kasich, Paul, Rubio
8 Manchester, NH 2/6/16 Bush, Carson, Christie, Cruz, Kasich, Rubio, Trump
9 Greenville, SC 2/13/16 Bush, Carson, Cruz, Kasich, Rubio, Trump
10 Houston, TX 2/25/16 Carson, Cruz, Kasich, Rubio, Trump
11 Detroit, MI 3/3/16 Cruz, Kasich, Rubio, Trump
12 Miami. FL 3/10/16 Cruz, Kasich, Rubio, Trump

Democratic Primary Debates

1 Las Vegas, NV 10/13/15 Chafee, Clinton, O'Malley, Sanders, Webb
2 Des Moines, IA 11/14/15 Clinton, O'Malley, Sanders
3 Manchester, NH 12/19/15 Clinton, O'Malley, Sanders
4 Charleston, SC 1/17/16 Clinton, O'Malley, Sanders
5 Durham, NY 2/4/16 Clinton, Sanders
6 Milwaukee, WI 2/11/16 Clinton, Sanders
7 Flint, MI 3/6/16 Clinton, Sanders
8 Miami, FL 3/9/16 Clinton, Sanders
9 Brooklyn, NY 4/14/16 Clinton Sanders

CHAPTER SIX

Primary Social Media

It is time to take back our country! Together we will make AMERICA SAFE & GREAT AGAIN! (Trump, Facebook, 2/1/15)

Far too many Republicans won't invest the political capital to nominate principled constitutionalists to the Supreme Court. I will. (Cruz, Facebook, 2/14/15)

I ran for president with the message that the government needs to once again work for the people, not the people work for the government. And while running for president I tried to reinforce what I have always believed—that speaking your mind matters, that experience matters, that competence matters and that it will always matter in leading our nation. (Christie, Facebook, 2/10/15)

Ted Cruz is a totally unstable individual. He is the single biggest liar I've ever come across, in politics or otherwise, and I have seen some of the best of him. His statements are totally untrue and completely outrageous. It is hard to believe that a person who proclaims to be a Christian could be so dishonest and lie so much. (Trump, Facebook, 2/15/15)

Campaign media accrete over time. In the beginning, American political candidates employed speeches and broadsides (posters); newspapers (many of which were affiliated with a political party) also printed stories about candidates for office. Over time additional media appeared and matured, allowing candidates to reach more voters and reinforce their campaign themes, so candidates added newspaper ads, direct mail pamphlets, radio ads, debates, television spots, campaign webpages, and email to their arsenal. Until recently, development of another medium simply mainly meant candidates had yet another channel to reach voters. Early candidate webpages resembled resumes (Benoit, 2000); as time went on, these websites became more sophisticated. Facebook emerged in 2004 and Twitter in 2006.

However, it is vital to understand that social media (particularly Twitter and Facebook) are more than simply additional media on which to place the basic ideas from speeches, debates, and webpages—they facilitate networks, connections among voters and candidates. Voters could tweet or retweet just as did the candidates; in contrast, citizens did not engage in televised debates or produce TV spots.

Twitter has differences from other media (see, e.g., Glantz & Benoit, 2018). In 2017, the permissible number of characters allowed in a tweet doubled from 140 to 280, but this medium still strictly limits the length of these messages. It is possible to spread a message over multiple tweets but the number of tweets required to convey the same ideas as a speech or debate would be ridiculous. Tweets also reach a more limited audience than other media such as TV spots or debates. The Twitter "audience" is self-selected; one must decide to follow a Twitter account (feed) in order to receive these messages. This means that Twitter can be an efficient way to reach core supporters. Other media, such as Facebook or the news media can repeat tweets and one Twitter user can re-tweet a message from another user, increase the reach of a tweet. Because it is self-selected, Twitter is better designed as medium for reaching supporters with succinct messages than to convey a complex message to a mass audience. During the 2016 presidential primary and general election campaigns the importance of Twitter skyrocketed. Donald Trump relied on Twitter and Facebook (and the free publicity from comments many thought were outrageous) to reach voters. Social media use by political candidates will never be the same.

The Nature and Importance of the Internet and Social Media

The 2016 presidential campaign demonstrated the importance of social media—particularly Twitter—as Donald Trump relied less on television spots and more on tweets than previous presidential candidates—or than his general election opponent Hillary Clinton. The Internet and the media which are enabled by the Internet have increased in reach and impact since its inception. In the U.S., about 25% of candidates had campaign websites in 2001; today, almost all candidates have a webpage (Gainous & Wagner, 2014). Worldwide, on August 13, 2017, over

1.2 billion webpages were available on the Internet and over 3.6 billion people accessed websites on the Internet (Internet Live Stats, 2017). Benoit and Glantz (2017) investigate attacks in 2016 Republican primary social media.

The Internet grew out of a Department of Defense contract for ARPANET (Advanced Research Projects Agency Network) in 1970 and commercial Internet Service providers were established in the 1980s (History of the Internet, 2016). The Internet grew rapidly, handling just 1% of the information moved through two-way telecommunications networks in 1993 but over 97% of such data in 2007 (History of the Internet). On August 13, 2017 over 3.9 billion Google searches occurred (Internet Live Stats, 2017).

The Internet facilitates use of social media, which includes a variety of platforms, including Facebook, Twitter, Instagram, and Snapchat. Gainous and Wagner (2014) explained that "each individual in a social network chooses whether to read, redistribute, or even add to each stream of information that comes to them" (p. 11). Use of social media contrasts sharply with traditional mass media. Auter and Fine (2016) noted that social media allow "politicians to maintain direct control of their messages to potential voters, bypassing the distortive gatekeeping function of media. Additionally, unlike costly national campaign tools, social media campaigning is cheap, requiring only the setup and maintenance of a (free) account" (p. 1000; see Gainous & Wagner, 2014). Notice that traditional media, such as TV spots or debates, do not create this type of network (users who can "read, redistribute… or add to" the information in the network). Interestingly, voters can use social media to redistribute, comment on, or add to traditional media such as TV spots or debates (see, e.g., Bramlett, McKinney, & Warner, 2018). Social media are an attractive way to reach voters.

Many Americans use social networking sites. In 2015, 76% of adults who were online used social networking sites (Pew, 2015). Facebook was used by 72% of online adults and Twitter by 23%. The Pew Research Center reports the number of people who participate in social media daily (2017). 76% of Facebook consumers employed this social media platform daily; 42% of those who use Twitter did so on a daily basis. Facebook pages have an average of 155 friends (Knapton, 2016); Twitter feeds have an average of 208 followers (Beevolve, 2017). The percentage of registered voters who follow feeds on social media sites such as Facebook and Twitter doubled from 2010 to 2014 (Anderson, 2015). Research by Nielsen (Casey, 2017) found that social media is widely used by older adults: "Surprisingly, the heavy social media user group isn't Millennials. In fact, Generation X (ages 35-49) spends the most time on social media: almost 7 hours per week versus Millennials, who come in second, spending just over 6 hours per week." Social media use increased from 3% of youth in 2005 to 86% in 2016. Pew also reported the percentage of youth who used different social media (2017). Facebook led the way with 88% of young social media users employing the platform. Instagram, Pinterest, and Linkedin, and Twitter were used by between 20 and 30% of youth.

Twitter

Twitter was launched in 2006 (Gainous & Wagner, 2014, p. 77). This program allows one user to follow another (somewhat similar to the friend feature in Facebook). A person creates a twitter feed and those who are interested can choose to follow it. Tweets are limited to 140 characters (although it is possible to generate several tweets on the same topic) and can include comments, links to webpages, pictures, and other content. Twitter recently increased the maximum number of characters to 280. 52% of users got news on Twitter in 2013; by 2015 it had increased to 63% (Lichterman, 2015). In 2012, "over 50,000 Obama-related tweets per minute" occurred during his nomination acceptance address (Gainous & Wagner, 2014, p. 6). Internet Live Stats reported that on August 13, 2017 over 477 million tweets were sent this day between over 309 million active Twitter users (2017). During the 2016 presidential primary and general election campaigns the importance of Twitter skyrocketed. Hillary Clinton's Twitter feed had 13.3 million followers in 2016; Trump's feed attracted 25.1 million followers. It is possible that some of these followers do not really exist (are fake accounts); still, it is clear that millions of people followed these candidates' Twitter feeds.

Twitter enables users to have a "dual screen" experience: watching one thing (such as a political debate) while tweeting or reading tweets from others. The statistic given earlier about Obama-related tweets during his acceptance address illustrates the dual media phenomenon. Dual-screen usage could mean less attention was paid to the debate but more attention was obtained from watching others' tweets.

Gainous and Wagner (2014) analyzed tweets from members of congress and leading candidates in the 2010 congressional elections. The most common topic of these message is campaign announcements (44%), followed about equally by character (19%), attacks (18%), and policy (17%). Challengers used Twitter more frequently than incumbents, 66% to 34% (Gainous & Wagner, 2014, p. 82). They also reported that Republicans tweeted more than Democrats and candidates for the Senate tweeted more frequently than candidates running for the House of Representatives.

In the 2016 presidential general campaign, the Democratic and Republican candidates employed Twitter in different ways: "Only Trump tended to include members of the public in his reposts: 78% of his retweets were from members of the public, compared with none of Clinton's and 2% of Sanders'" (Pew, 2016). The Republican's approach could well have had the effect of making his followers feel valued (if Mr. Trump retweeted my tweet, it must be important) and feel as if they were part of the campaign, part of the on-going "conversation." Another contrast is that most of Trump's tweets linked to news media stories; the majority of Clinton's tweets linked to her webpage (Pew, 2016).

Facebook

Facebook was launched in 2004 (History of Facebook, 2017). It was designed to connect Harvard students, but by 2006 it was open to everyone (at least 13 years old with an email address). Auter and Fine (2016) analyzed the Facebook posts of all Senate candidates in 2010. They confirmed several factors that influence the amount of negative posts. Competitive races produced more attacks than non-competitive races. Trailing candidates made more posts than leading candidates. Overall, negative posts addressed issues over twice as much as character. Competitive races produced more issue attacks than non-competitive campaigns. Finally, trailing candidates were more likely to attack than leading candidates.

Borah (2016) analyzed presidential candidates' Facebook pages from 2008 (Obama vs. McCain) and 2012 (Obama vs. Romney). Overall, acclaims were more common than attacks (59% to 41%); however, the two Republican candidates attacked more than they acclaimed. Obama utilized more appeals to enthusiasm; McCain and Romney relied most heavily on fear appeals. She found most posts served to promote the campaigns. Policy was the second most common type of post; no instances of posts on character occurred. Obama deployed more acclaims than his opponents, while McCaim and Romney attacked more that Obama. Shen and Benoit (2016) examined the Facebook pages of Obama and Romney in the 2012 general election campaign. Acclaims were the most common function (60%), followed by attacks (39%), and defenses (1%). Policy was about three times as common as character (76% to 24%). In 2016 Clinton and Trump used Facebook differently. "78% of Trump's links in Facebook posts send readers to news media stories while 80% of Clinton's direct followers to campaign pages" (Pew, 2016). These candidates' Facebook pages offered different kinds of information to users.

Sample

The sample of tweets and Facebook posts analyzed here was obtained from the 2016 presidential election campaigns (January 15–February 15; six candidates suspended their campaigns during this period, so the sample is smaller for them: Chris Christie, Carly Fiorina, Jim Gilmore, Mike Huckabee, Martin O'Malley, Rand Paul, and Rick Santorum). From the Democratic primary, Clinton, O'Malley, and Sanders were included; from the GOP primary, Bush, Carson, Christie, Cruz, Fiorina, Gilmore, Huckabee, Kasich, Paul, Rubio, Santorum, and Trump comprised the sample. The sample of Facebook pages included the same three Democrats and Republicans Bush, Christie, Cruz, Gilmore, Kasich, Rubio, and Trump.

Results

As predicted, both tweets and Facebook posts used acclaims the most and attacks the least: Tweets 71% acclaims, 28% attacks, and 1% defenses; Facebook 72% acclaims, 27% attacks, and 1% defenses. Defenses were obviously the least common function (combined 72%, 27%, 1%). A significant difference occurred in the distribution of acclaims and attacks (χ^2 [$df = 1$] = 1178.87, $p < .0001$). Only Bernie Sanders' tweets attacked more than they acclaimed. For example, Clinton touted her goal of "end-to-end reform in our criminal justice system" in a tweet (February 17, 2016). Donald Trump's Facebook page promised that he would "MAKE AMERICAN GREAT AGAIN!" (February 15, 2015). Rubio's Facebook posts included this acclaim: "Marco Rubio has a plan to counter Russian aggression" (February 15, 2015). These excerpts illustrate the use of social media to acclaim. These data are reported in Table 6.1.

The candidates' social media also included examples of attacks. For example, a post on Kasich's Facebook feed attacked a fellow Republican: "Jeb Bush is fizzling out" (January 23, 2015). Cruz's Facebook account included criticism of Donald Trump's consistency: "Donald J. Trump: 'I'm very capable of changing to anything I want to change to'" (February 15, 2015). Another example of an attack appeared on Sanders' Facebook page (February 15, 2015) criticized the opposing party: "Republicans are waging a war against women." Social media were used to attack in the 2016 presidential primary campaign.

Defenses can also be found in the candidates' social media. Clinton explained that she did not simply support Obama to win African–American votes: "#POTUS' achievements speak for themselves. The idea that [my] supporting him is a ploy to win black votes is baffling" (February 17, 2016). Trump's Facebook page also offered a defense (February 15, 2015): "Cruz said I would be appointing a liberal judge when in fact I will appoint a great conservative." Examples of the three functions appear in these texts.

Table 6.1. Functions and Topics of 2016 Presidential Social Media.

	Functions			Topics	
	Acclaims	Attacks	Defenses	Policy	Character
Twitter					
Clinton	**556 (72%)**	212 (27%)	5 (0.4%)	**448 (58%)**	320 (42%)
O'Malley	**49 (78%)**	14 (22%)	0	**44 (70%)**	19 (30%)
Sanders	189 (43%)	**249 (57%)**	0	**356 (81%)**	82 (19%)
Democratic	**794 (62%)**	475 (37%)	3 (0.2%)	**848 (67%)**	421 (33%)
Bush	**391 (69%)**	171 (30%)	2 (0.4%)	271 (48%)	**291 (52%)**
Carson	**234 (85%)**	39 (14%)	2 (1%)	105 (38%)	**168 (62%)**
Christie	**128 (70%)**	54 (30%)	0	27 (15%)	**155 (85%)**
Cruz	**509 (78%)**	139 (21%)	5 (1%)	201 (31%)	**447 (69%)**
Fiorina	**36 (69%)**	16 (31%)	0	11 (21%)	**41 (79%)**
Gilmore	**68 (92%)**	6 (8%)	0	34 (46%)	**40 (54%)**
Huckabee	**48 (71%)**	20 (29%)	0	23 (34%)	**45 (66%)**
Kasich	**342 (94%)**	22 (6%)	1 (0.3%)	144 (40%)	**220 (60%)**
Paul	**104 (58%)**	73 (41%)	1 (0.6%)	71 (40%)	**106 (60%)**
Rubio	**189 (83%)**	36 (16%)	2 (1%)	48 (21%)	**177 (79%)**
Santorum	**51 (96%)**	0	2 (4%)	18 (35%)	**33 (65%)**
Trump	**242 (54%)**	183 (41%)	20 (4%)	43 (10%)	**382 (90%)**
Republican	**2342 (75%)**	759 (24%)	35 (1%)	996 (32%)	**2105 (68%)**
Twitter Total	**3136 (71%)**	1234 (28%)	38 (1%)	1844 (42%)	**2526 (58%)**
Facebook					
Clinton	**218 (73%)**	81 (27%)	1 (0.3%)	122 (41%)	**177 (59%)**
O'Malley	**33 (83%)**	7 (18%)	0	16 (40%)	**24 (60%)**
Sanders	**161 (60%)**	102 (38%)	5 (2%)	**137 (52%)**	126 (48%)
Democrats	**379 (67%)**	183 (32%)	6 (1%)	259 (46%)	**303 (54%)**
Bush	**150 (74%)**	52 (26%)	1 (0.5%)	63 (31%)	**139 (69%)**
Christie	**59 (71%)**	20 (24%)	4 (5%)	17 (22%)	**62 (78%)**
Cruz	**82 (73%)**	28 (25%)	2 (2%)	34 (31%)	**76 (69%)**
Gilmore	**30 (91%)**	3 (9%)	0	9 (27%)	**24 (73%)**
Kasich	**244 (79%)**	63 (21%)	0	93 (30%)	**214 (70%)**
Rubio	**91 (75%)**	28 (23%)	2 (2%)	22 (18%)	**97 (82%)**
Trump	**127 (76%)**	39 (23%)	2 (1%)	72 (43%)	**94 (57%)**
Republicans	**783 (76%)**	233 (23%)	10 (1%)	310 (31%)	**706 (69%)**
Facebook Total	**1162 (73%)**	416 (26%)	16 (1%)	569 (36%)	**1009 (64%)**
Grand Total	**4298 (72%)**	1650 (27%)	54 (1%)	2413 (41%)	**3535 (59%)**

Acclaims vs. Attacks: χ^2 (df = 1) = 1178.87, p < .0001
Topics: χ^2 (df = 1) = 211.65, p < .0001

These social media messages did not confirm the second hypothesis: policy constituted 41% of themes whereas character comprised 59% of statements. This contrast was significant, but in the opposite direction from the prediction (χ^2 [*df* = 1] = 211.65, $p < .0001$). Each Republican candidate stressed character over policy for both Twitter and Facebook. The story on the Democratic side was not consistent. Clinton, O'Malley, and Sanders all emphasized policy in their tweets; only Sanders stressed policy on Facebook. For example, Rubio's Facebook posts discussed policy: "While Obama & Clinton have tried to appease Russia, I've consistently laid out a plan to counter Putin's aggression" (February 15, 2015). Another post about policy can be found on O'Malley's Facebook page: "We must put more cops on the Wall St. beat. A crime is a crime, whether it's committed on Wall Street or Main Street" (January 31, 2015). Santorum's Facebook page addressed foreign policy: "If ISIS wants to form a 7th century caliphate, then the solution is simple: Let's bomb them back to the 7th century" (January 29). These examples illustrate how social media can address policy. These data are also displayed in Table 3.1.

Social media discussed character as well. Christie's Facebook posts stressed his leadership ability (a character trait): "Chris Christie has the extensive executive and leadership experience that our country needs" (Facebook, January 25, 2015). Carson discussed his personal qualities in a Facebook post: "The American people deserve leaders that conduct themselves with integrity, civility, and honesty" (February 15, 2015). These three traits—integrity, civility, honesty—clearly concern character. A Facebook post from Trump asserted his independence: "The only people I owe are the voters" (January 25, 2015). This statement clearly does not concern policy, only his character. So, both policy and character are encompassed by these social media messages.

Research question 1 addressed the forms of policy. In these data, 34% of these were about past deeds, 2% concerned future plans, and 64% addressed general goals. This distribution was statistically significant (χ^2 [*df* = 2] = 1351.01, $p < .0001$). H3 held that general goals would be used more often for acclaims than attacks. This prediction was upheld (χ^2 [*df* = 1] = 721.45, $p < .0001$). See Table 6.2 for these data.

Research question 2 concerned the forms of character. Forms of character were distributed with 58% on personal qualities, 17% about leadership ability, and 25% on ideals. This division of forms of character is statistically significant (χ^2 [*df* = 2] = 721.45, $p < .0001$). The fourth hypothesis anticipated that ideals would be used more frequently in acclaims than attacks. This prediction was confirmed in this sample (χ^2 [*df* = 1] = 524.97, $p < .0001$). These data are reported in Table 6.4.

Table 6.2. Target of Attack in 2016 Social Media.

	Own Party	Other Party
Twitter		
Clinton	37	93
O'Malley	0	7
Sanders	0	34
Democrats	37 (22%)	**134 (78%)**
Cruz	4	49
Fiorina	5	6
Gilmore	3	1
Huckabee	1	12
Kasich	2	5
Paul	5	44
Rubio	1	28
Santorum	0	0
Trump	10	10
Republicans	43 (14%)	**265 (86%)**
Facebook		
Clinton	38	42
O'Malley	5	1
Sanders	34	26
Democrats	**77 (53%)**	69 (47%)
Bush	47	7
Christie	9	4
Cruz	13	5
Gilmore	1	1
Kasich	66	3
Rubio	18	11
Trump	19	2
Republicans	**171 (84%)**	33 (16%)
Grand Total	328 (40%)	**501 (60%)**

Table 6.3. Forms of Policy in 2016 Presidential Social Media.

	Past Deeds		Future Plans		General Goals	
	Acclaims	Attacks	Acclaims	Attacks	Acclaims	Attacks
Twitter						
Clinton	34	96	15	6	256	41
	130 (29%)		21 (5%)		297 (66%)	
O'Malley	3	4	4	0	26	7
	7 (16%)		4 (9%)		33 (75%)	
Sanders	3	181	3	0	145	24
	184 (52%)		3 (1%)		169 (47%)	
Democratic	40	281	22	6	427	72
	321 (38%)		28 (3%)		499 (59%)	
Bush	53	45	7	0	134	32
	98 (36%)		7 (3%)		166 (61%)	
Carson	0	7	1	0	89	8
	7 (7%)		1 (1%)		97 (92%)	
Christie	14	2	0	0	10	1
	16 (59%)		0		11 (41%)	
Cruz	8	41	1	0	112	39
	49 (24%)		1 (0.5%)		151 (75%)	
Fiorina	0	3	0	0	5	3
	3 (27%)		0		8 (73%)	
Gilmore	0	0	0	0	34	0
	0		0		34 (100%)	
Kasich	59	7	1	0	75	2
	66 (46%)		1 (1%)		77 (53%)	
Paul	3	11	0	1	38	18
	14 (20%)		1 (1%)		56 (79%)	
Rubio	5	13	0	0	25	5
	18 (38%)		0		30 (63%)	
Santorum	8	0	0	0	10	0
	8 (44%)		0		10 (56%)	
Trump	0	8	0	0	22	13
	8 (19%)		0		35 (81%)	
Republicans	153	141	10	1	562	129
	294 (30%)		11 (1%)		691 (69%)	
Total Twitter	193	422	32	7	989	201
	615 (33%)		39 (2%)		1190 (65%)	

(continued)

Table 6.3. *continued*

	Past Deeds		Future Plans		General Goals	
	Acclaims	Attacks	Acclaims	Attacks	Acclaims	Attacks
Facebook						
Clinton	16	15	2	3	69	17
	31 (25%)		5 (4%)		86 (70%)	
O'Malley	0	1	4	0	0	10
	1 (7%)		4 (27%)		10 (67%)	
Sanders	7	42	2	1	69	16
	49 (36%)		3 (2%)		85 (62%)	
Democratic	23	57	4	4	138	33
	80 (31%)		8 (3%)		171 (66%)	
Bush	24	11	4	0	23	1
	35 (56%)		4 (6%)		24 (38%)	
Christie	2	8	1	0	6	0
	10 (59%)		1 (6%)		6 (35%)	
Cruz	0	6	1	0	23	4
	6 (18%)		1 (3%)		27 (79%)	
Gilmore	0	0	0	0	9	0
	0		0		9 (100%)	
Kasich	32	17	5	0	38	1
	49 (53%)		5 (5%)		39 (42%)	
Rubio	0	8	1	1	11	1
	8 (36%)		2 (9%)		12 (55%)	
Trump	0	16	0	0	56	0
	16 (22%)		0		56 (78%)	
Republican	58	66	12	1	166	7
	124 (40%)		13 (4%)		173 (56%)	
Facebook Total	81	123	16	5	304	40
	204 (36%)		21 (4%)		344 (60%)	
Grand Total	274	545	48	12	1293	241
	819 (34%)		60 (2%)		1534 (64%)	

Forms of Policy: χ^2 (df = 2) = 1351.01, $p < .0001$
Functions of General Goals: χ^2 (df = 1) = 721.45, $p < .0001$

Table 6.4. Forms of Character in 2016 Presidential Social Media.

	Personal Qualities		Leadership Ability		Ideals	
	Acclaims	Attacks	Acclaims	Attacks	Acclaims	Attacks
Twitter						
Clinton	98	44	73	9	80	16
	142 (44%)		82 (26%)		96 (30%)	
O'Malley	5	2	3	0	8	1
	7 (37%)		3 (16%)		9 (47%)	
Sanders	5	29	3	2	30	13
	34 (41%)		5 (6%)		43 (52%)	
Democratic	108	75	79	11	118	30
	183 (43%)		90 (21%)		148 (35%)	
Bush	95	67	57	15	45	12
	162 (56%)		72 (25%)		57 (20%)	
Carson	56	13	10	1	78	10
	69 (41%)		11 (7%)		88 (52%)	
Christie	69	43	16	8	19	0
	112 (72%)		24 (15%)		19 (12%)	
Cruz	209	41	37	2	142	16
	250 (55%)		39 (9%)		168 (37%)	
Fiorina	13	7	4	0	14	3
	20 (49%)		4 (10%)		17 (41%)	
Gilmore	10	5	9	1	15	0
	15 (38%)		10 (25%)		15 (38%)	
Kasich	95	8	60	5	52	0
	103 (47%)		65 (30%)		52 (24%)	
Paul	22	30	1	8	40	5
	52 (49%)		9 (8%)		45 (42%)	
Rubio	67	7	15	11	77	0
	74 (42%)		26 (15%)		77 (44%)	
Santorum	20	0	2	0	11	0
	20 (61%)		2 (6%)		11 (33%)	
Trump	193	148	15	141	12	0
	341 (67%)		156 (31%)		12 (2%)	
Republicans	874	373	226	67	517	48
	1247 (59%)		293 (14%)		565 (27%)	
Twitter Total	982	448	305	78	635	78
	1430 (57%)		383 (15%)		713 (28%)	

(continued)

Table 6.4. *continued*

	Personal Qualities		Leadership Ability		Ideals	
	Acclaims	Attacks	Acclaims	Attacks	Acclaims	Attacks
Facebook						
Clinton	76	39	37	4	18	3
	115 (65%)		41 (23%)		21 (12%)	
O'Malley	7	4	5	1	7	0
	11 (46%)		6 (25%)		7 (29%)	
Sanders	48	36	7	1	28	6
	84 (67%)		8 (6%)		34 (27%)	
Democratic	124	75	44	5	46	9
	199 (66%)		49 (16%)		55 (18%)	
Bush	39	27	38	6	22	7
	66 (47%)		44 (32%)		29 (21%)	
Christie	34	10	13	2	3	0
	44 (71%)		15 (24%)		3 (5%)	
Cruz	26	14	7	0	25	4
	40 (53%)		7 (9%)		29 (38%)	
Gilmore	13	3	6	0	2	0
	16 (67%)		6 (25%)		2 (8%)	
Kasich	80	38	73	7	16	0
	118 (55%)		80 (37%)		16 (7%)	
Rubio	38	14	12	2	29	2
	52 (54%)		14 (14%)		31 (32%)	
Trump	59	21	6	0	6	2
	80 (85%)		6 (6%)		8 (9%)	
Republican	289	127	155	17	103	15
	416 (59%)		172 (24%)		118 (17%)	
Facebook Total	413	202	199	22	149	24
	615 (61%)		221 (22%)		173 (17%)	
Grand Total	1395	650	504	100	784	102
	2045 (58%)		604 (17%)		886 (25%)	

Forms of Character: χ^2 (df = 2) = 721.45, p < .0001
Functions of Ideals: χ^2 (df = 1) = 524.97, p < .0001

Discussion and Conclusion

These data provide an insight into a new and important medium: social media. The messages in this sample confirm to Hypothesis 1: acclaims were more common than attacks which in turn occurred more often than debates. Functional Theory explains this prediction by observing that acclaims have no particular drawbacks (although this does not mean acclaims are automatically persuasive). Attacks run the risk of alienating some voters who dislike mudslinging. Defenses are expected to be the least common function for three reasons: defenses may suggest that the candidate is reactive instead of proactive, defenses generally take a candidate off-message, and the only way to defend against a particular attack is to identify it and then refute it; mentioning the attack could inform or remind voters of a possible weakness of the candidate. These results are consistent with most research using the Functional approach. They are also consistent with Shen and Benoit's (2016) findings on general presidential Facebook pages from 2012.

In their social media posts, these candidates again attacked members of their own party as well as members of the opposition party. However, in social media the other party received more attacks than fellow party members.

The second hypothesis was not supported: Policy did not occur more often than character; in fact, character was more common than policy in most of these messages. This result is not consistent: Some candidates stressed policy whereas others emphasized character. Most past research on Functional Theory (Benoit, 2007), as well as analysis of general presidential Facebook pages from 2012 (Shen & Benoit, 2016) found policy was usually more prevalent than character. The emphasis on character could stem from the fact that social media are relatively new; Benoit (2000) found early candidate webpages emphasized character more than policy. Later studies of candidate Internet sites found the emphasis shifted toward policy (Benoit, Glantz, & Rill, 2016; Benoit, Henson, Davis, Glantz, Phillips, & Rill, 2013). The only way to answer this question is to study the topics of future social media messages.

Another possible explanation for the failure to confirm hypothesis two is the idea that social media are a more personal medium than other message forms. Acceptance Addresses, which celebrate the candidate, tend to emphasize character more than other media, such as TV spots or debates. The comparatively more personal nature of social media could encourage stress on character.

These social media were prone to base more acclaims than attacks on general goals (H3) and ideals (H4). Functional Theory argues that most goals (such as keeping America safe) and ideals (such as justice) lend themselves more to acclaiming than attacking. These data shed light on a relatively new and increasingly important way to connect candidates and voters: social media.

CHAPTER SEVEN

Primary TV Talk Shows

> Do we want to support a campaign that is based on—on yelling and screaming and cursing and insults? Or do we wanna unify behind a positive, optimistic, forward-looking, conservative campaign, based on real policy solutions to the problems facing this country. (Ted Cruz, *Meet the Press*, May 1, 2016)

> We have to deal in a very substantive way with income and wealth inequality. We need to understand why we're the only major country on Earth not to guarantee health care to all people, not to have paid family and medical leave. And that we have to deal aggressively with a corrupt campaign finance system which allows big money interest to buy elections. (Bernie Sanders, *Meet the Press*, May 1, 2016)

> When people make these kinds of claims [that do not want to work against climate change], which now I think I have been debunked; actually *The Washington Post* said three Pinocchios, *The New York Times* also analyzed it, and other independent analysts have said that they are misrepresenting my record. (Hillary Clinton, *Meet the Press*, May 1, 2016)

> Marco Rubio has the worst voting record in the United States Senate in many, many years. He doesn't even show up to vote. He's defrauded the people of Florida. He won't even show up to vote. (Donald Trump, *Meet the Press*, March 13, 2016)

Daytime television Talk shows have been around for decades. *Meet the Press* and *Face the Nation* debuted in the 1950s. More recently they have been used by presidential candidates as another way to reach potential voters. The Functional Theory of Political Campaign Discourse has been used to investigate TV talk show appearances by candidates in the 2000 (Benoit, McHale, Hansen, Pier, & McGuire, 2003) and 2004 (Benoit, Stein, McHale, Chattopaddhyay, Verser, and Price, 2007) presidential campaigns. This chapter extends that work to the 2016 presidential primary campaign.

Literature Review

This medium has been investigated in two presidential campaigns. Research on both 2000 (Benoit, McHale, Hansen, Pier, & McGuire, 2002) and 2004 (Benoit, Stein, McHale, Chattopaddhyay, Verser, and Price, 2007) had found that acclaims were the most common function (72%, 68%), followed by attacks (17%, 31%), and then by defenses (12%, 1%). Unlike most message forms, television talk show appearances stressed character (65% in each) more than policy (35% in each). A contrast emerged in target of attack: in 2000 78% of attacks were directed toward other members of the same party and 22% criticized the opposing party; in 2004 (when only the Democratic Party held primaries) 20% of attacks targeted other Democrats and 90% attacked the Republican Party. In 2000 discussion of general goals predominated policy statements (75%), with past deeds (15%) and future plans (10%) occurring much less frequently. In 2004, past deeds (49%) and general goals (46%) occurred at roughly the same rate; future plans (5%) comprised a small portion of policy statements. In both 2000 (75%) and 2004 (68%) constituted the bulk of character utterances. Leadership ability accounted for 7% of these statements in 2000 and 28% in 2004; ideals made up 18% of character statements in 2000 and 4% in 2004. In both campaigns, general goals were used more often as the basis of acclaims than attacks; the same can be said of ideals in these two campaigns.

Sample

Texts were obtained for two Democrats—Clinton and Sanders—on *Meet the Press* and *Face the Nation*. We located texts for Bush, Cruz, Kasich, Paul, Rubio, and Trump on *Meet the Press* and for Christie, Cruz, Kasich, Paul, Rubio, and Trump on *Face the Nation*. These texts were content analyzed with the same procedures employed in the two prior studies of TV talk shows as well as in the other chapters in this book.

Results

In these texts acclaims were the most common function (45%), followed by attacks (37%), and then defenses (19%). This contrast was statistically significant (χ^2 [df = 1] = 16.44, $p < .0001$). Cruz illustrated an acclaim when he declared on *Face the Nation* that he was running on "jobs and freedom and security and protecting the American people" (May 1, 2016). These goals (and one value, freedom) are likely to viewed as favorable by most voters, making them acclaims. Bernie Sanders appealed to Democratic voters with these acclaims: I will "demand that the wealthy and large corporations start paying their fair share of taxes" (May 1, 2016).

Lindsey Graham criticized Donald Trump when he declared that "Donald Trump's foreign policy is isolationism. It will lead to another 9/11" (May 1, 2016). September 11 saw terrorist attacks (via commercial airliners) so this statement must be viewed as an attack. When discussion campaign donations, Clinton characterized Sanders' remarks as "a very artful smear" (February 7, 2016). Suggestion that her primary opponent attempted to smear her reputation illustrates a character attack.

Hillary Clinton (March 6, 2016) provided an example of a defense when she responded to concerns about her private email server: "Remember I'm the one who asked that all my e-mails be made public. I have been more transparent than anybody I can think of in public life." The appearance of transparency mitigates against the accusations against her. Donald Trump responded to concerns about his failure to release his tax returns: "When you're under audit, you don't give your papers" (February 28, 2016). This defense appeals to defeasibility, arguing that he was not allowed to release his taxes. See Table 7.1 for these data.

Both Democrats and Republicans, on both *Meet the Press* and *Face the Nation* attacked their own party (73%) more than the opposition party (27%). A *chi-square goodness of fit* test revealed that this difference was significant (χ^2 [df = 1] = 170.71, $p < .0001$). These data are displayed in Table 7.2.

Character was more common than policy in these texts (56% to 44%). This difference was significant, but in the opposite direction from the prediction (χ^2 [df = 1] = 21.09, $p < .0001$).

Clinton discussed her plans to regulate banking: "I rolled out the toughest, most effective effort to rein in financial abuse of anybody in this campaign.... It does into shadow banking. It goes after hedge funds. It goes after the carried interest loophole" (February 7, 2016). Proposals for banking regulations illustrate a policy statement. Trump announced that: "I'm very much into the military, and will build our military bigger, better, stronger than ever before" (January 31, 2016). This statement addresses his policy. On the other hand, Trump criticized Ted

Table 7.1. Functions and Topics of 2016 in 2016 TV Talk Show Appearances.

	Functions			Topics	
	Acclaims	Attacks	Defenses	Policy	Character
Meet the Press					
Clinton	**63 (60%)**	24 (23%)	18 (17%)	43 (49%)	**44 (51%)**
Sanders	**101 (51%)**	78 (39%)	21 (11%)	**108 (60%)**	71 (40%)
Democrats	**164 (54%)**	102 (33%)	39 (13%)	**151 (57%)**	115 (43%)
Bush	8 (40%)	**12** (60%)	0	2 (10%)	18 (90%)
Cruz	64 (38%)	**83** (50%)	20 (12%)	39 (26%)	**112 (74%)**
Kasich	**63 (60%)**	24 (23%)	18 (17%)	36 (43%)	**48 (57%)**
Paul	9 (27%)	**18** (55%)	6 (18%)	16 (59%)	11 (41%)
Rubio	24 (33%)	**31** (43%)	17 (24%)	23 (42%)	**32 (58%)**
Trump	78 (34%)	68 (30%)	**81 (36%)**	71 (49%)	**75 (51%)**
Republicans	**250 (41%)**	233 (38%)	127 (21%)	187 (39%)	**296 (61%)**
Total	**414 (45%)**	335 (37%)	166 (18%)	338 (45%)	**411 (55%)**
Face the Nation					
Clinton	**52 (59%)**	21 (24%)	15 (17%)	**47 (64%)**	26 (36%)
Sanders	**110 (50%)**	68 (31%)	44 (20%)	**75 (88%)**	10 (12%)
Democrats	**162 (52%)**	89 (29%)	59 (19%)	**150 (60%)**	101 (40%)
Christie	**7 (44%)**	3 (19%)	6 (38%)	4 (40%)	**6** (60%)
Cruz	**68 (46%)**	66 (45%)	14 (9%)	42 (31%)	**92** (69%)
Kasich	**72 (63%)**	33 (29%)	9 (8%)	**75 (87%)**	11 (13%)
Paul	4 (27%)	**10** (67%)	1 (7%)	7 (50%)	7 (50%)
Rubio	31 (28%)	**63 (57%)**	16 (15%)	23 (24%)	**71 (76%)**
Trump	**142 (39%)**	117 (32%)	109 (30%)	100 (39%)	**159** (61%)
Republicans	**324 (42%)**	292 (38%)	155 (20%)	206 (33%)	**420 (67%)**
Total	**486 (45%)**	381 (35%)	214 (20%)	356 (41%)	**521 (59%)**
Grand Total	**900 (45%)**	736 (37%)	380 (19%)	744 (44%)	**932 (56%)**

Total Acclaims vs. Attacks: χ^2 (df = 1) = 16.44, $p < .0001$
Total Topics 2016: χ^2 (df = 1) = 21.09, $p < .0001$ (in the opposite direction from prediction)

Cruz's character "I think Ted Cruz has been severely affected by the Goldman Sachs loans, which he didn't disclose" (January 31, 2016). This attack does not concern Senator Cruz's banking policy, but a personal loan, so it addresses character. Marco Rubio accused Cruz of making "disingenuous attacks" (January 31, 2016). This characterization does not flatter his opponent's character. These data are also displayed in Table 7.1

These candidates' TV talk show appearances stressed general goals (50%) and past deeds (42%) when they discussed policy. Future plans accounted for

Table 7.2. Target of Attack in Primary TV Talk Shows.

	Own Party	Other Party
Meet the Press		
Clinton	7	12
Sanders	29	0
Democrats	**36 (75%)**	12 (25%)
Bush	9	1
Cruz	64	21
Kasich	9	5
Paul	14	5
Rubio	14	10
Trump	36	20
Republicans	**146 (66%)**	74 (34%)
Total	**182 (68%)**	86 (32%)
Face the Nation		
Clinton	15	3
Sanders	27	13
Democrats	42 (72%)	16 (28%)
Christie	2	1
Cruz	62	6
Kasich	26	6
Paul	5	0
Rubio	61	5
Trump	58	21
Republicans	**214 (85%)**	39 (15%)
Total	**396 (76%)**	125 (24%)
Grand Total	**578 (73%)**	211 (27%)

Target of Attacks: χ^2 ($df = 1$) = 170.71, $p < .0001$

8% of statements. This contrast is statistically significant (χ^2 [$df = 2$] = 107.7, $p < .0001$). When the candidates discussed general goals, they were far more likely to make acclaims than attacks (χ^2 [$df = 1$] = 63.96, $p < .0001$). See Table 7.3 for these data.

This study also investigated the three forms of character. Most such statements concerned personal qualities (78%) when about the same number of character statements on ideals (12%) and leadership ability (10%). These differences were significant (χ^2 [$df = 2$] = 366.76, $p < .0001$). When they discussed ideals, candidates showed a pronounced proclivity for acclaims than attacks (χ^2 [$df = 1$] = 21.33, $p < .0001$). See Table 7.4 for these data.

Table 7.3. Forms of Policy in 2016 in 2016 TV Talk Show Appearances.

	Past Deeds		Future Plans		General Goals	
	Acclaims	Attacks	Acclaims	Attacks	Acclaims	Attacks
Democrats	15	38	11	8	68	10
Republicans	14	82	3	6	75	26
2016 Total	29	120	14	14	143	36
	149 (42%)		28 (8%)		179 (50%)	

Form of Policy: χ^2 (df = 2) = 107.7, $p < .0001$
Functions of General Goals: χ^2 (df = 1) = 63.96, $p < .0001$

Table 7.4. Forms of Character in 2016 TV Talk Show Appearances.

	Personal Qualities		Leadership Ability		Ideals	
	Acclaims	Attacks	Acclaims	Attacks	Acclaims	Attacks
Democrats	56	30	7	3	5	0
Republicans	178	156	19	14	35	8
2016 Total	134	186	26	17	40	8
	320 (78%)		43 (10%)		48 (12%)	

Forms of Character: χ^2 (df = 2) = 366.76, $p < .0001$
Functions of Ideals: χ^2 (df = 1) = 21.33, $p < .0001$

Discussion and Conclusion

These presidential primary TV talk show appearances conformed to most, but not all, predictions. The three functions occurred in the predicted order. This finding is consistent with Functional Theory and the research on this message form in 2000 and 2004. Attacks focused on other members of the attacking candidate's political party, which is consistent with past studies on this message form. However, these texts discussed character more than policy. Functional Theory does not insist that every candidate must emphasize policy, only that they have reasons to do so and often do so. This pattern—greater emphasis on character than policy—occurred in the TV talk shows from the 2000 and 2004 campaigns. Apparently, TV talk shows are more of a personal medium than, say, TV spots or debates.

These messages discussed future plans infrequently, as past research found. General goals were the basis of more acclaims than attacks, as predicted by H3. Character comments tended to center on personal qualities, like other message forms. As predicted in H4, ideals were used more often to acclaim than attack. More research on this type of message could prove fruitful.

CHAPTER EIGHT

Nomination Acceptance Addresses

Decades of progress made in bringing down crime are now being reversed by this Administration's rollback of criminal enforcement. Homicides last year increased by 17 percent in America's fifty largest cities. That's the largest increase in 25 years. In our nation's capital, killings have risen by 50 percent. They are up nearly 60 percent in nearby Baltimore. In the President's hometown of Chicago more than 2,000 people have been the victims of shootings this year alone. And almost 4,000 have been killed in the Chicago area since he took office. The number of police officers killed in the line of duty has risen by almost 50 percent compared to this point last year. Nearly 180,000 illegal immigrants with criminal records, ordered deported from our country, are tonight roaming free to threaten peaceful citizens. The number of new illegal immigrant families who have crossed the border so far this year already exceeds the entire total from 2015. They are being released by the tens of thousands into our communities with no regard for the impact on public safety or resources. (Trump, Acceptance Address, July 21, 2015)

We will lead our party back to the White House, and we will lead our country back to safety, prosperity, and peace. We will be a country of generosity and warmth. But we will also be a country of law and order. (Trump, Acceptance Address, July 21, 2015)

Donald Trump… spoke for 70-odd minutes—and I do mean odd. And he offered zero solutions. But we already know he doesn't believe these things. No wonder he doesn't like talking about his plans. (Clinton, Acceptance Address, July 28, 2015)

> In my first 100 days, we will work with both parties to pass the biggest investment in new, good-paying jobs since World War II. Jobs in manufacturing, clean energy, technology and innovation, small business, and infrastructure. If we invest in infrastructure now, we'll not only create jobs today, but lay the foundation for the jobs of the future. (Clinton, Acceptance Address, July 28, 2015)

Political campaign discourse is unquestionably goal-directed: intended to secure the candidate's election to office (a few candidates run to champion a cause, of course). This chapter extends the work on the functions of political campaign discourse generally—and the 2016 Acceptance Addresses specifically—by analyzing the functions and topics of acceptance addresses in the 2016 presidential election campaign. We briefly review the literature on acceptance addresses. The we report the data from 2016 acceptances, and then we consider the implications of this content analysis.

Nomination Acceptance Addresses

The presidential nominating convention acceptance address is a form of campaign discourse that gradually emerged in the early part of the 19th century (Trent & Friedenberg, 2004). Nominees responded to the nomination with formal letters and telegrams of acceptance. Twenty years later, Democratic candidates responded with informal speeches and Democrat Horatio Seymour delivered the first formal acceptance address in 1868, albeit not delivered at the nomination convention. In 1932, Franklin Roosevelt broke with tradition by attending the Democratic national convention in Chicago, the first presidential candidate to accept his nomination in person at the convention. From this point on the acceptance speech has become an integral part of the convention process.

The presidential nomination acceptance address is an extremely important discourse form. First, by accepting the party's nomination, the nominee brings the primary contest to a close. The nominations in both political parties was hotly contested in 2016. Bernie Sanders did not endorse Hillary Clinton until July 12 roughly two weeks before her nomination address of July 28; a vocal "Stop Trump" movement continued until the delegates' voters were cast at the Republican National Convention on July 19. This means the primary phase dragged out longer than usual in 2016. The nominees' acceptance addresses seek to celebrate or rebuild their parties' unity and appeal to voters as yet undecided; it celebrates the political party, its ideals, and the nominee's candidacy. Second, these speeches culminate the quadrennial gathering of the major political parties. The acceptance address is meant to climax the rituals performed and witnessed by the party faithful. Thousands of party members gather to enthusiastically participate in these dramatic acts at the conventions, and millions more watch the spectacle at home. Trump's speech attracted 34.9 million viewers; whereas Clinton's acceptance was watched by 33.3 million people (Huddleston, 2016). A third reason to study acceptance addresses is the fact that about a quarter of the electorate decides how to vote during the party nominating conventions (Holbrook, 1996)—we concede this percentage may be smaller today than it was 20 years ago, but these messages still reach, and could affect, millions of voters. We also note that an important effect of political campaigns is to reinforce rather than to change vote preference. The stronger a person's vote intention, the more likely he or she is to persist in this attitude, actually cast a vote on election day, donate to the preferred candidate, and talk up their candidate with others. Finally, the nominees enact the transition to the general election campaign, often providing a preview of the key themes they plan to develop during that campaign (Trent & Friedenberg, 1995). In contested primaries the candidates appeal to members of their party; in the general election the candidates must broaden their message so as to attract other voters. Therefore, this recurrent form of campaign discourse merits scholarly attention.

Benoit, Wells, Pier, and Blaney (1999) examined the functions and topics of Acceptance Addresses from 1960 to 1996 (speeches from 1952 and 1956 were analyzed subsequently). Acclaims were the dominant function (72%) followed by attacks (27%); defenses were rare (1%). These speeches discussed policy (56%) than character (44%). In 2000 (Benoit, McHale, Hansen, Pier, & McGuire, 2003), the Acceptances were comprised entirely of acclaims (89%) and attacks (11%). Policy was more common than character (55% to 45%). The Acceptance Addresses from 2004 have also been content analyzed (Benoit, Stein, McHale, Chattopadhyay, Verser, & Price, 2007). Acclaims were most common 72%, followed by attacks 27%, and then defenses at 1%. Policy was again somewhat more common than (55%) character (45%). Benoit (2014b) examined these speeches from the 2008 and 2012 elections. Once again acclaims were the most common function (73%), followed by attacks (27%), and defenses (0.5%). Policy and character occurred at nearly the same frequency (policy 52%, character 48%). These speeches were quite similar over time, with roughly 3/4 of themes acclaims, 1/4 attacks, and 1% or less defenses. Policy and character occurred at about the same rate with a bit of emphasis on policy (around 55% policy to 45% character). This study extends Functional Analysis to the 2016 Acceptance Addresses by Donald Trump and Hillary Clinton (traditionally the nominating convention for the challenging party occurs earlier than the convention for the incumbent party).

Sample

This chapter is limited to the Democratic and Republican nomination acceptance addresses. Traditionally, the challenging party holds its convention first. Therefore, because Democrat Barack Obama was the sitting president, Republican Donald Trump delivered his nomination acceptance speech on July 21, 2016 in Cleveland, OH. Hillary Clinton, the Democratic nominee, gave her acceptance address on July 28, 2016 in Philadelphia, PA.

Results

The first hypothesis predicted that acclaims would be more common than attacks, which in turn will be more common than defenses. This hypothesis was confirmed: These speeches contained 61% acclaims, 39% attacks, and 0.5% defenses. Acclaims were used significantly more often than attacks (χ^2 [df = 1] = 18.44, p < .0001). Trump provided an example of an acclaim when he declared that "We will lead our country back to safety, prosperity, and peace. We will be a country of generosity and warmth. But we will also be a country of law and order" (2016). Notice that this remark touches on both policy (safety, prosperity, peace, law and order) and character (generosity, warmth) and all of these ideas would surely be viewed positively by his audience. Clinton included this acclaim in her acceptance: "We will build an economy where everyone who wants a good paying job can get one. And we'll build a path to citizenship for millions of immigrants who are already contributing to our economy!" (2016). Creating jobs is a goal that would appeal to any voter; a path to citizenship for immigrants would likely be endorsed by most Democrats. These data are reported in Table 8.1.

These speeches also include attacks. For instance, Clinton (2016) "Now Donald Trump says, and this is a quote, 'I know more about ISIS than the generals

Table 8.1. Functions and Topics of 2016 Presidential Nomination Acceptance Addresses.

	Functions			Topics	
	Acclaims	Attacks	Defenses	Policy	Character
Clinton	**133 (75%)**	42 (24%)	2 (1%)	67 (38%)	**108 (62%)**
Trump	97 (47%)	**111 (53%)**	0	**142 (68%)**	66 (32%)
2016 Total	**239 (61%)**	153 (39%)	2 (0.5%)	**209 (55%)**	174 (45%)

Acclaims vs. Attacks: χ^2 (df = 1) = 18.44, p < .0001
Topics: χ^2 (df = 1) = 3.2, *ns*

do....' No, Donald, you don't. He thinks that he knows more than our military because he claimed our armed forces are 'a disaster.'" This remark could be seen to criticizes the GOP nominee in two ways: He has a huge ego, he lacks leadership ability. Trump (2016) illustrated an attack when he charged that

> After four years of Hillary Clinton [as Secretary of State], what do we have? ISIS has spread across the region, and the entire world. Libya is in ruins, and our Ambassador and his staff were left helpless to die at the hands of savage killers. Egypt was turned over to the radical Muslim brotherhood, forcing the military to retake control. Iraq is in chaos. Iran is on the path to nuclear weapons. Syria is engulfed in a civil war and a refugee crisis now threatens the West. After fifteen years of wars in the Middle East, after trillions of dollars spent and thousands of lives lost, the situation is worse than it has ever been before. This is the legacy of Hillary Clinton: death, destruction, terrorism and weakness.

He accuses his opponent of multiple foreign policy failures in this remark, a clear example of an attack (well, multiple attacks). Defenses were rare in these addresses, but we can find an example in Clinton's acceptance: "I'm not here to repeal the 2nd Amendment. I'm not here to take away your guns" (Clinton, 2016). This utterance defends against the charge that the Democratic nominee is anti-gun, denying this allegation.

H2 anticipated that these speeches would address policy more than character. Combined, the two nominees addressed policy more than character (55% to 45%), which was not a significant difference (χ^2 [*df* = 1] = 3.2, *ns*). These data can also be found in Table 8.1.

An example of an utterance the addresses policy can be found in Clinton's (2016) acceptance:

> In my first 100 days, we will work with both parties to pass the biggest investment in new, good-paying jobs since World War II. Jobs in manufacturing, clean energy, technology and innovation, small business, and infrastructure. If we invest in infrastructure now, we'll not only create jobs today, but lay the foundation for the jobs of the future. And we will transform the way we prepare our young people for those jobs.

Job creation is a clear illustration of a policy comment (and this utterance is also an acclaim). Trump (2016) provided another example of a statement on policy (although this one is an attack): "This Administration has failed America's inner cities. Remember, it has failed America's inner cities. It's failed them on education. It's failed them on jobs. It's failed them on crime. It's failed them in every way and on every single level." Education, jobs, and crime are all illustrations of policy.

The GOP nominee criticized his opponent's character when he stated that "When that same Secretary of State rakes in millions of dollars trading access and favors to special interests and foreign powers I know the time for action has come." (2016). "Pay to Play" (charging for access to a politician) and doing favors for special interests are certain to be viewed unfavorably. If Trump had identified, for example, favors for specific special interests (say, banking interests) that would move the attack into the realm of policy. Clinton (2016) touted her leadership ability, illustrating a character comment: "I've been your First Lady. Served 8 years as a Senator from the great State of New York.... Then I represented all of you as Secretary of State." These—particularly the last two—are indicative of her experience in office or leadership ability.

Research question 2 concerned the relative frequency of the three forms of policy. These speeches discussed general goals most often when addressing policy (56%), followed by past deeds (41%), with few future plans discussed (3%). These differences were statistically significant (χ^2 [$df = 2$] = 91.01, $p < .0001$). The third hypothesis predicted that general goals would be used more often in acclaims than

Table 8.2. Forms of Policy in 2016 Presidential Nomination Acceptance Addresses.

	Past Deeds		Future Plans		General Goals	
	Acclaims	Attacks	Acclaims	Attacks	Acclaims	Attacks
Clinton	2	11	4	0	46	4
Trump	0	73	1	2	57	9
2016 Total	2	84	5	2	103	13
	86 (41%)		7 (3%)		116 (56%)	

Forms of Policy: χ^2 ($df = 2$) = 91.01, $p < .0001$
Functions of General Goals: χ^2 ($df = 1$) = 68.28, $p < .0001$

Table 8.3. Forms of Character in 2016 Presidential Nomination Acceptance Addresses.

	Personal Qualities		Leadership Ability		Ideals	
	Acclaims	Attacks	Acclaims	Attacks	Acclaims	Attacks
Clinton	35	11	14	16	32	0
Trump	27	20	4	7	8	0
2016 Total	62	31	18	23	40	0
	93 (53%)		41 (24%)		40 (23%)	

Forms of Character: χ^2 ($df = 2$) = 31.69, $p < .0001$
Functions of Ideals: χ^2 ($df = 1$) = 38.02, $p < .0001$

attacks. This was confirmed: 103 acclaims (89%) and 13 attacks (11%) concerned general goals (χ^2 [df = 1] = 68.28, $p < .0001$). These data can be found in Table 8.2.

RQ3 concerned the relative frequency of the three forms of character. Personal qualities comprised 53% of character comments, 24% of these themes were about leadership ability, and 23% discussed ideals. As was the case with forms of policy, the forms of character occurred with different frequencies (χ^2 [df = 2] = 31.69, $p < .0001$; it is clear that leadership ability and ideals occurred with about the same frequency). The fourth prediction addressed use of ideals in these speeches. Utterances about ideals were exclusively acclaims (40 acclaims, 0 attacks). Not surprisingly, these frequencies were significantly different (χ^2 [df = 1] = 38.02, $p < .0001$). These data are provided in Table 8.3.

Discussion and Conclusions

Functional Theory predicts that acclaims are likely to be more common than attacks. This was the case overall in 2016 as it has been in previous Acceptance Addresses (Benoit, 2014b; Benoit, Wells, Pier, & Blaney, 1999). However, Clinton clearly stressed acclaims more than attacks, whereas Trump's speech was more evenly balanced (with a few more attacks than acclaims). Trump was viewed by some as very negative; this perception could be in part a contrast effect. In this speech Trump was slightly more negative than positive, but he attacked significantly more than his opponent, Clinton.

Past research into Acceptance Addresses revealed that Democrats tend to discuss policy more, and character less, than Republicans (Benoit, 2014b; Benoit, Wells, Pier, & Blaney, 1999). In 2016, this distribution was reversed, with the Democrat discussing character more than policy and the Republican discussing policy more than character. This could reflect the candidates' opportunities to discuss character. Apparently Clinton saw more opportunities to attack Trump's character than his policy proposals (which were not laid out in as much detail as Clinton's ideas).

As predicted, both general goals and ideals served as the foundation for acclaims more often than for attacks. This is consistent with Functional Theory predictions and past research on Acceptances (Benoit, 2014b; Benoit, Wells, Pier, & Blaney, 1999).

This study provided a systematic analysis of the functions of Donald Trump's and Hillary Clinton's presidential nomination acceptance addresses from the 2016 presidential campaign. Analysis of this group of texts revealed that nominees frequently engaged in acclaiming and attacking, along with a few instances of defense. Combined, the two speeches used more acclaims than attacks (and few defenses). This finding is consistent with Functional Theory. Acclaims have no inherent drawbacks. Attacks, in contrast, could damage the attacker with tse voters who dislike mudslinging. Defenses have three drawbacks, which means they should be the least common function: defenses could foster the impression that the defender is more indicative that the candidate is reactive instead of proactive. If attacks tend to stress a candidate's weaknesses, defending against an attack could shift a candidate off-message. Finally, before one can defend against a particular criticism, one must mention the attack, which could inform or remind voters of a potential weakness.

Although not predicted, the data reveal that Trump used attacks more (53% to 24%), and acclaims less, than Clinton (47% to 75%; χ^2 [df = 1] = 18.44, $p < .0001$). This could be because Trump was trying to appeal to his base. It is also possible that he was more prone to use insults than his opponent.

These speeches did not conform to the second hypothesis: No significant difference was found in the use of policy versus character. This could be due to the fact that, like social media, nomination acceptance addresses are more personal—more about character—than other media such as TV spots or debates. Further analysis revealed that Trump stressed policy more than Clinton (χ^2 [df = 1] = 34.46, $p < .0001$, φ =.3). Trump never held elective office, so he did not have a record (policy) to attack. It appears to us that the Republican did not elaborate his policy proposals as fully as the Democrat, which again left Clinton with less policy to attack. In contrast, Trump repeatedly attacked on past deeds, mostly targeting Obama directly and Clinton by implication.

As predicted by H3 (on general goals) and by H4 (on ideals), more acclaims than attacks used these topics. It is easier to acclaim goals, such as helping the poor, or ideals, such as freedom, than to attack them.

CHAPTER NINE

General Television Spots

Introduction

> I'm voting for respect... I'm voting for courage. (Clinton, "Roar," 2016)

> Decades of lies, cover-ups and scandal have finally caught up with Hillary Clinton. (Trump, "Unfit," 2016)

> Donald Trump. His plan: Lower taxes. Families get childcare tax credits. Law and Order, balanced with justice and fairness, and America is respected in the world again. (Trump, "United," 2016)

> How do we make the economy work for everyone? Hillary Clinton's plan starts here, by making big corporations and those at the top finally pay their fair share in taxes. And those companies that move overseas, she'd charge them an exit tax. Then she'd use that money to make the largest investment in creating good paying jobs since World War II. Millions of jobs. You can read the plan here. (Clinton, "How To," 2016)

Political advertising is used by political candidates to reach voters. In primary elections, ads are not broadcast in every state; they are plentiful in upcoming primary and caucus states. In the general election political commercials for presidential candidates air in battleground states, where the likely winner (who receives the electoral votes) is as yet in doubt. Candidates spend millions of dollars running thousands of spots. This exposure—typically repeated because a given ad is usually broadcast multiple times—guarantees that many citizens view these messages and therefore could be influenced by television advertising.

Benoit, Leshner, and Chattopadhyay (2007) used meta-analysis to cumulate the research on the effects of viewing political campaign TV spots. Television advertising does not affect everyone, or course. Nor does it necessarily affect all viewers in the same way. Nevertheless, watching election ads significantly increased issue knowledge, altered perceptions of candidate character, changed attitudes, altered candidate preference, changed likelihood that the viewer would vote, and had an agenda-setting effect (issues discussed in ads became more important to viewers). This ubiquitous message form merits scholarly attention.

Literature Review

Research has investigated political television advertising. The first presidential ads were broadcast in the 1952 presidential campaign and have been an important component of political campaigns ever since (Benoit, 2014a). Research on presidential spots has established that acclaims are more common than attacks; defenses generally account for only about 1% of themes in these messages (Benoit, 2014a). Candidate commercials address policy more often than character. A detailed review of research on political television advertising can be found in Benoit (2014a).

Sample

This study focused on candidate-sponsored TV spots in the 2016 general election presidential campaign. It includes 35 advertisements from Hillary Clinton, 13 commercials from Donald Trump, 22 from pro-Clinton or Anti-Trump groups, and 11 from pro-Trump or anti-Clinton groups. The candidate ads totaled 48; spots sponsored by groups totaled 33.

Results

These television commercials were roughly equally divided between acclaims (46%) and attacks (54%) with no defenses. In this sample, attacks were more common than acclaims; however, this contrast was not statistically significant

Table 9.1. Functions and Topics of 2016 General TV Spots.

	Functions			Topics	
	Acclaims	Attacks	Defenses	Policy	Character
Clinton	61 (41%)	**88 (59%)**	0	40 (27%)	**109 (73%)**
Trump	27 (48%)	**29 (52%)**	0	**33 (59%)**	23 (41%)
Total	88 (43%)	**117 (57%)**	0	73 (36%)	**132 (64%)**
Groups	23 (14%)	**137 (86%)**	0	36 (23%)	**124 (78%)**

Candidates: Acclaims vs. Attacks: χ^2 (*df* = 1) = 1.96, *ns*
Acclaims vs. Attacks for Candidates vs. Groups: χ^2 (*df* = 1) = 34.62, $p < .0001$, $\varphi = .31$
Candidates: Topics χ^2 (*df* = 1) = 16.98, $p < .0001$

([*df* = 1] = 1.96, *ns*). Accordingly, H1 on the functions of these messages was not confirmed. These data are displayed in Table 9.1.

Examples of acclaims can be found in these texts. For instance, Trump declares that "My childcare plan allows for every family in American to deduct their childcare expenses from their income taxes" (Trump, "Listening," 2016). This goal is likely to be viewed positively by many voters. Trump also touted tax cut proposal: "You get a 20% tax rate reduction" (Trump, "Consumer Benefit," 2016). Clinton acclaimed when one of her spots explained that "Under her plan, working parents get relief from the costs of child care and a path to debt-free college. Equal pay for women and paid time off to care for family" (Clinton, "For Those Who Depend on Us," 2016). Again, help with child care expenses is likely to be viewed favorably by many people; she adds goals of support for college, equal pay for women, and time to provide family care would likely appeal to her target audience.

Attacks can also be found in these texts. For instance, this spot for the GOP candidate asserted that "Hillary Clinton doesn't have the fortitude, strength, or stamina to lead our world" (Trump, "Dangerous," 2016). This theme criticizes Clinton's leadership ability. Clinton attacked Trump's arrogance: Brzezinski: "Who are you consulting with…so you're ready on Day One?" Trump: "I'm speaking with myself…. My primary consultant is myself" (Clinton, "Myself," 2016). The world, including American, is so complex no single person can be an expert on everything. Trump asserted that "In Hillary Clinton's America: The middle class gets crushed…spending goes up… taxes go up… Hundreds of thousands of jobs disappear" (Trump, "Two Americas: Economy," 2016). Increased government spending, higher taxes, and lost jobs are undesirable outcomes for many. These excerpts illustrate attacks in 2016 general presidential TV spots.

The second hypothesis concerns the distribution of topics in these campaign messages. Policy occurred less than character (36–64%). Analysis revealed that these frequencies are significantly different (χ^2 [df = 1] = 16.98, $p < .0001$), but in the opposite direction anticipated. H2 was therefore not confirmed here. These data are also reported in Table 9.1.

One of the Republican candidate's ads addressed his tax policy, discussing specific future plans:

> What does electing Donald Trump president mean for you? Families making sixty thousand a year: You get a twenty percent tax rate reduction. Working moms: You get paid maternity leave and an average $5,000 childcare tax reduction. Business owners: Your taxes get cut from thirty-five to fifteen percent so you can expand and create more jobs. (Trump, "Two Americas: Economy," 2016)

Trump's proposals for tax cuts, paid maternity leave, childcare deduction are likely to appeal to many in his audience, along with his goal of creating jobs. Clinton aired a spot that also discussed policy: "Hillary Clinton's plan starts here, by making big corporations and those at the top finally pay their fair share in taxes. And those companies that move overseas, she'd charge them an exit tax. Then she'd use that money to make the largest investment in creating good paying jobs since World War II. Millions of jobs" (Clinton, "How To," 1952). Many voters would approve of making the rich pay more in taxes, punishing companies that moved out of the U.S., and creating jobs.

Other commercials addressed character. Trump argued that "Staggering amounts of cash poured into the Clinton Foundation from criminals, dictators, countries that hate America. Hillary cut deals for donors" (Trump "Corruption," 2016). Notice this criticism does not focus on her policies—such as taxes, education, or immigration—but her character, suggesting corruption. The Democratic nominee questioned Trump's character while boasting Clinton's character:

> Cindy Guerra: "I became active in the Republican Party to elect Ronald Reagan. I thought I would be able to support whoever the Republican candidate was. I always have. But with Trump on the ballot, I just can't. He does not hold my values or the values of the party. He's unfit, he's unqualified. And I see Hillary Clinton as someone who's had the experience nationally and internationally to be our leader." (Clinton, "Values," 2016)

This excerpt questions the Republican's values (ideals) and his leadership ability while praising Clinton's leadership ability.

The first research question concerned the distribution of the three forms of policy. In these data, past deeds comprised 32% of policy utterances, future plans were 7%, and general goals constituted 60% of policy comments. This distribution was statistically significant (χ^2 [df = 2] = 40.69, $p < .0001$). See Table 9.2 for these data. Hypothesis 3 had to do with the use of general goals to acclaim or attack. This prediction was not confirmed (χ^2 [*df* = 1] = 2.38, *ns*). These data are also in Table 9.3.

The second research question concerned the distribution of character utterances. Most were about the candidates' personal qualities (64%) with 21% on leadership ability and 15% about ideals. These frequencies were significantly different (χ^2 [*df* = 2] = 87.26, $p < .0001$). These data are shown in Table 9.2. The fourth hypothesis concerned the functions of utterances on ideals. Ideals were used more often as the basis of acclaims than attacks (χ^2 [*df* = 1] = 11.27, $p < .005$). These data are also reported in Table 9.3.

The final hypothesis tested with these data had to do with the source of utterances. H4 anticipated that ads sponsored by groups would contain fewer acclaims and more attacks than ads from candidates. Group ads did acclaim less (14–43%) and attack more (86% to 57%) than candidate spots in this sample. This contrast was significant (χ^2 [*df* = 1] = 34.62, $p < .0001$, $\varphi = .31$). These data can also be found in Table 9.1.

Table 9.2. Forms of Policy in 2016 General TV Spots.

	Past Deeds		Future Plans		General Goals	
	Acclaims	Attacks	Acclaims	Attacks	Acclaims	Attacks
Clinton	18	0	2	0	12	8
Trump	0	6	5	0	14	8
Total 2016	18	6	7	0	26	16
	31 (32%)		7 (7%)		58 (60%)	

Forms of Policy: χ^2 (*df* = 2) = 40.69, $p < .0001$
General Goals 2016: χ^2 (*df* = 1) = 2.38, *ns*

Table 9.3. Forms of Character in 2016 General TV Spots.

	Personal Qualities		Leadership Ability		Ideals	
	Acclaims	Attacks	Acclaims	Attacks	Acclaims	Attacks
Clinton	7	66	12	13	10	1
Trump	3	11	1	4	4	0
Total 2016	10	77	13	17	14	1
	131 (64%)		43 (21%)		31 (15%)	

Forms of Character: χ^2 (*df* = 2) = 87.26, $p < .0001$
Functions of Ideals: χ^2 (*df* = 1) = 11.27, $p < .005$

Discussion and Conclusions

Functional Theory argues that acclaims will be more common than attacks in this message form. Past studies of General TV Spots confirm this prediction. In these data, no significant difference occurred. We observe that Functional Theory does not assert that candidates *must* acclaim more than they attack, only that reasons exist for not stressing attacks. Individual candidates may detest their opponent so much they cannot help attacking. Some people are simply malevolent, and such candidates may naturally attack in their messages. It is also possible that a candidate does not fully appreciate the risks of backlash from attacks and so do not try to moderate their criticisms. There is no way to determine why these two candidates attacked so much.

The general campaign ads in 2016 stressed character more than policy, inconsistent with Functional Theory and past research (see, e.g., Benoit, 2014a). Closer inspection of Table 9.1 reveals a contrast between candidates in their topic emphasis. Clinton discussed character more, and policy less, than Trump (χ^2 [df = 1] = 16.98, $p < .0001$). Again, Functional Theory does not declare that candidates *must* address policy more than character, only that they have reasons to do so. In 2016, Trump had no political record, having never been elected to public office (he boasted of his prowess as a business magnate but such comments do not qualify as "policy"). This means that Trump had no past deeds for Clinton to attack. She may have decided to criticize his character instead. Again, there is no way to know for certain why candidates choose the topics they stress.

H3, on functions of general goals, was not confirmed. General goals were used more often to acclaim than attack (26 to 16) but with this sample size the contrast is not significant. These data did confirm H4, on the functions of ideals. Functional Theory argues that ideals, such as justice or freedom, are easier to acclaim than to attack. These data add to our understanding of presidential TV spots.

CHAPTER TEN

General Debates

We have to build an economy that works for everyone, not just those at the top. That means we need new jobs, good jobs, with rising incomes. I want us to invest in you. I want us to invest in your future. That means jobs in infrastructure, in advanced manufacturing, innovation and technology, clean, renewable energy, and small business, because most of the new jobs will come from small business. We also have to make the economy fairer. That starts with raising the national minimum wage and also guarantee, finally, equal pay for women's work. (Clinton, Debate 1, 2016)

Our jobs are fleeing the country. They're going to Mexico. They're going to many other countries. You look at what China is doing to our country in terms of making our product. They're devaluing their currency, and there's nobody in our government to fight them. And we have a very good fight. And we have a winning fight. Because they're using our country as a piggy bank to rebuild China, and many other countries are doing the same thing. So we're losing our good jobs, so many of them.... Under my plan, I'll be reducing taxes tremendously, from 35 percent to 15 percent for companies, small and big businesses. That's going to be a job creator like we haven't seen since Ronald Reagan. It's going to be a beautiful thing to watch. Companies will come. They will build. They will expand. New companies will start. And I look very, very much forward to doing it. We have to renegotiate our trade deals, and we have to stop these countries from stealing our companies and our jobs. (Trump, Debate 1, 2016)

Do the thousands of people that you have stiffed over the course of your business not deserve some kind of apology from someone who has taken their labor, taken the

> goods that they produced, and then refused to pay them? And when we talk about your business, you've taken business bankruptcy six times. (Clinton, Debate 1, 2016)

> Typical politician. All talk, no action. Sounds good, doesn't work. Never going to happen. Our country is suffering because people like Secretary Clinton have made such bad decisions in terms of our jobs and in terms of what's going on. (Trump, Debate 1, 2016)

The first debate of 2016 was watched by a huge audience: 84 million (Grynbaum, 2016; the audience was actually larger, because this figure does not include those who watched on C-SPAN or via the Internet). The previous record was 1980, when Jimmy Carter and Ronald Reagan only had one general election debate, which was watched by 80 million people. The first debate between Obama and Trump in 2012, by contrast, attracted 67 million viewers. A large percentage of the American public watched debates in 2016. The three general presidential debates of 2016 combined reached over 222 million viewers (Koblin, 2016).

Although the first debate of 2016 enjoyed the largest audience for these debates in history, earlier debates were also watched by many people. The combined audience for general election debates is huge: "The Commission on Presidential Debates (2012) reports that the average viewership of general election debates from 1960 to 2008 is 59 million.... The grand total for viewers of all presidential and vice presidential debates exceeds one billion through 2012" (Benoit, 2014c, p. 5). The large size of the audience means a correspondingly large potential for influencing voters.

Benoit, Hansen, and Verser (2003) report a meta-analysis of the effects of watching debates. Debates increase viewers' issue knowledge, issue salience (number of issues important to viewer), and preference for candidates' policy positions. These events have agenda-setting effects: The issues discussed in debates become more important to viewers. Debates influence perceptions of candidate character (they can enhance or detract from a candidates' character). Debates can alter vote preferences. Of course, watching debates do not change the beliefs and attitudes of all viewers, but they affect a significant number of citizens. Debates can also reinforce attitudes, which can have several beneficial effects for candidates: increasing supporters' likelihood of (1) donating money to the candidate; (2) talking the candidate up with friends, family, and co-workers; and (3) actually voting on election day.

Debates are an important message form for several reasons. As noted, they attract the attention of millions of voters and they have significant effects on voters. Debates are important for voters because they allow citizens to directly compare and contrast the leading candidates usually addressing the same questions.

An election is a choice between candidates or parties and the best way to choose is to compare the alternatives. The face-to-face confrontation of debates is important because it can produce clash between the leading candidates' ideas, helping voters learn more than they might from highly scripted speeches or TV spots. The rules for political campaign debates usually prohibit candidates from bringing prepared notes into the encounter. This can mean that unexpected questions or comments from opponent may provoke more candid answers than what occurs in heavily scripted spots or speeches. Debates also provide extended exposure to candidates: Debates are longer than most other campaign messages (in 1960, the four debates were 60 minutes in length; debates since then have been 90 minutes in length) and some elections feature more than one debate. For candidates, debates are an additional medium for appealing to voters, one with a huge audience and virtually no cost to candidates (unlike television spots, for example).

In 2016, the general election debates featured Hillary Clinton and Donald Trump. They engaged in three debates; their vice presidential candidates, Tim Kaine and Mike Pence, participated in one debate. This study reports a content analysis of these messages employing the the Functional Theory of Political Campaign Discourse (Benoit, 2007). Next, we report the results. Then we discuss the findings and implications of this study.

Results

The first hypothesis held that acclaims would be more common than attacks, and that defenses were the least common function. Inspection of Table 10.1 reveals

Table 10.1. Functions and Topics of 2016 General Campaign Debates.

	Functions			Character	
	Acclaims	Attacks	Defenses	Policy	Character
Clinton	**288 (50%)**	219 (39%)	58 (10%)	**285 (56%)**	227 (44%)
Trump	216 (32%)	368 **(54%)**	100 (15%)	**300 (56%)**	240 (44%)
Presidential	504 (40%)	**587 (47%)**	158 (13%)	**585 (56%)**	467 (44%)
Kaine	121 (42%)	**152 (52%)**	18 (6%)	124 (45%)	**149 (55%)**
Pence	101 (38%)	**123 (46%)**	45 (17%)	**152 (68%)**	72 (32%
VP Debates	222 (40%)	**275 (49%)**	63 (11%)	**276 (56%)**	221 (44%)

Presidential acclaims vs. attacks χ^2 (df = 1) = 7.86, $p < .05$ (not in predicted direction); Vice Presidential acclaims vs. attacks: χ^2 (df = 1) = 5.65, $p < .05$ (not in predicted direction)
Presidential topics: χ^2 (df = 1) = 13.24, $p < .0005$; Vice Presidential topics: χ^2 (df = 1) = 6.09, $p < .05$

that defenses were the least common function. However, attacks (47%) were more common than acclaims (40%) in presidential debates; attacks comprised 49% of the themes in vice presidential debates while acclaims were 40%. Vice presidential debates follow the same pattern. It is clear that H1 was not confirmed in this sample (Clinton was an exception).

We want to illustrate the three functions with utterances from this sample (these examples appeared in the last presidential debate). Clinton declared that "It is important that we not reverse marriage equality, that we not reverse Roe v. Wade, that we stand up against Citizens United, we stand up for the rights of people in the workplace." These statements were likely to be perceived positively for many (albeit not many conservatives; however, candidates do not need to persuade all voters of their preferability). Trump asserted that "I want to build a wall.... We stop the drugs... One of my first acts will be to get all of the drug lords, all of the bad ones.... out." These proposals would appeal to voters in his target audience, meaning that they are acclaims.

The Republican nominee criticized his opponent by observing that "She wants open borders. People are going to pour into our country. People are going to come in from Syria. She wants 555% more people than Barack Obama." These declarations were surely not meant as compliments. The Democrat argued that her opponent had "started his campaign bashing immigrants, calling Mexican immigrants rapists and criminals and drug dealers." This utterance serves as another example of an attack.

Defenses also were used in this confrontation. After Trump charged that Clinton would open our borders, she replied "We will not have open borders. This is a rank mis-characterization." This remark denies her opponent's accusation. Similarly, after Clinton suggested that Trump would be Putin's puppet, the GOP nominee declared "No puppet. No puppet." This statement exemplifies a defense, denying Clinton's criticism.

H2 expected that these four candidates would focus more on policy than character. This hypothesis was confirmed (χ^2 [df = 1] = 13.24, $p < .0003$). Clinton and Trump did not differ in their emphasis on the two topics, 56% acclaims and 44% attacks. However, Kaine made more attacks (55% to 32%) and fewer acclaims than Pence (45%, 68%). Previous presidential debates focused even more on policy than the 2016 debates (χ^2 [df = 1] = 169.9, $p < .0001$, $\varphi = .13$). The data from vice presidential debates are generally consistent. These data are also displayed in Table 10.1.

The first RQ investigated the relative frequency of the three forms of policy: past deeds, future plans, and general goals. In 2016, most policy statements addressed general goals (63%), followed by past deeds (32%) and future plans (5%).

Vice presidential debates followed the same pattern. H3 predicted that general goals would be used more often to acclaim than to attack. This prediction was confirmed: acclaims (78%), attacks (22%). This difference was statistically significant (χ^2 [df = 1] = 42.12, p < .0001). See Table 10.2 for these data.

Table 10.2. Forms of Policy in 2016 General Campaign Debates.

	Past Deeds		Future Plans		General Goals	
	Acclaims	Attacks	Acclaims	Attacks	Acclaims	Attacks
Clinton	29	34	25	20	154	23
Trump	0	159	6	7	97	31
Presidential	29	193	31	27	251	54
	222 (38%)		58 (10%)		305 (52%)	
Kaine	20	8	2	1	50	43
Pence	8	45	0	0	62	37
Vice Presidential	28	53	2	1	112	80
	81 (29%)		3 (1%)		192 (70%)	

Presidential Forms of Policy: χ^2 (df = 2) = 152.04, p < .0001; Vice Presidential Forms of Policy: χ^2 (df = 2) =196.11, p < .0001
Functions of General Goals Presidential: χ^2 (df = 1) = 127.96, p < .0001; Functions of General Goals Vice Presidential: χ^2 (df = 1) = 5.33, p < .05

Table 10.3. Forms of Character in 2016 General Campaign Debates.

	Personal Qualities		Leadership Ability		Ideals	
	Acclaims	Attacks	Acclaims	Attacks	Acclaims	Attacks
Clinton	46	121	17	20	22	2
Trump	47	115	10	56	12	0
Presidential	93	236	27	76	34	1
	329 (70%)		103 (22%)		35 (7%)	
Kaine	14	84	26	14	7	2
Pence	15	27	11	13	5	1
Vice Presidential	29	111	39	27	12	3
	140 (63%)		66 (30%)		15 (7%)	

Presidential Forms of Character: χ^2 (df = 2) = 304.36, p < .0001; Vice Presidential Forms of Character: χ^2 (df = 2) = 107.25, p < .0001
Functions of Ideals Presidential: χ^2 (df = 1) = 31.13, p < .0001; Functions of Ideals Vice Presidential: χ^2 (df = 1) = 5.4, p < .05

RQ2 concerns the relative emphasis on the three forms of character in the 2016 American presidential debates. The most common form of character is personal qualities, accounting for two-thirds (67%) of character utterances. The candidates' leadership ability was discussed in 20% of character themes. Ideals was the least common form of character at 15%. The same pattern occurred in vice presidential debates. Hypothesis four anticipated that ideals would be used for acclaims more often than for attacks. Statistical analysis confirmed this prediction (χ^2 [*df* = 1] = 23.00, $p < .0001$). These data are reported in Table 10.3.

Discussion and Conclusion

Overall, these two candidates attacked more than they acclaimed. However, Clinton acclaimed more (50% to 32%) and attacked less (39% to 54%) than Trump (χ^2 [*df* = 1] =42.89, $p < .0001$). Functional Theory does not make predictions for individual candidates, only for groups of candidates. There is no way to know why the GOP nominee attacked so much in these debates. The vice presidential candidates also favored attacks. They may have been acting as surrogates (Chapters 4 and 8 showed that group-sponsored ads attack more than candidate-sponsored ads), which could have led them to attack.

Both Clinton and Trump stressed policy over character, as expected. So did the vice presidential candidates in their debate. However, another contrast between the two political parties emerged as Kaine stressed character more, and policy less, than Pence (χ^2 [*df* = 1] = 25.08, $p < .0001$). Kaine may have believed character to be more important than policy, or perhaps he deemed the GOP opponents to be more vulnerable on character than policy.

Functional Theory predictions were confirmed on the functions of general goals and ideals. Both presidential and vice presidential debates used acclaims more than attacks when addressing goals and ideals. Most goals, such as reducing inflation or reducing the national debt, are easier to acclaim than to attack. The same can be said of ideals such as virtue or morality; easier to acclaim than attack.

CHAPTER ELEVEN

General Social Media

> Four hundred pieces of legislation have Hillary Clinton's name on them. (Clinton, Twitter, October 9, 2016)

> Hillary is the most corrupt person to ever run for the presidency of the United States. (Trump, Twitter, October 18, 2016)

> We're going to make public colleges tuition-free for families making less than $125,000 a year and debt-free for everyone else. (Clinton, Twitter, October 28, 2016)

> I am going to repeal and replace ObamaCare. We will have much less expensive and MUCH better healthcare. (Trump, Twitter, November 2, 2016)

> Between the three presidential debates, Trump told one lie for every 50 seconds he spoke. (Clinton, Twitter, October 20, 2016)

> My words [*Access Hollywood* video] were unfortunate—the Clintons' actions were far worse. (Trump, Twitter, October 8, 2016)

Chapter 6 discussed social media, arguing that both Twitter and Facebook are increasingly important campaign tools. Social media were also an important medium for reaching voters in the general election campaign in 2016. An early study undertook a Functional analysis of Facebook pages in the 2012 general election campaign. Shen and Benoit (2016) Obama's and Romney's Facebook pages. These messages followed expectations established in Functional Theory. They relied more on acclaims (60%) than attacks (25%) or defenses (0.2%). They both stressed policy (76%) over character (24%) on their Facebook pages. The candidates were also more likely to acclaim than attack when discussing general goals and ideals. This study employed Hillary Clinton's and Donald Trump's Twitter feeds and Facebook pages during the general election campaign (mid-August through election day).

Results

The first hypothesis, that acclaims will outnumber attacks, was not confirmed: 48% acclaims, 51% attacks, and defenses 1%. In fact, this distribution was significant in the opposite direction from this prediction (χ^2 [df = 1] = 5.41, $p < .05$). An example of an acclaim appears in this tweet from Trump: "If I am elected President, I am going to keep RADICAL ISLAMIC TERRORISTS OUT of our country" (Trump, Facebook, October 27). Everyone would agree that we should keep terrorists out of the country, although not everyone would agree with the sentiment implied about people who profess Islamic. Clinton offered another illustration of an acclaim when she outlined a general goal in a tweet: "I'll work to raise the minimum wage" (Hillary Clinton, Facebook, November 1). This idea would probably sound good to many people (many messages are controversial or divisive; increasing the minimum wage would not appeal to all voters). These data are displayed in Table 11.1.

An example of an attack on occurs in this excerpt from Clinton's Facebook account which declares that Trump is guilty of "demeaning, objectifying, and insulting women" (Hillary Clinton, Facebook, November 4). Many people dislike people who treat women this way, making this an attack. Trump predicted that "With Hillary, costs [of healthcare] will triple!" (Donald Trump, Facebook, November 2). Few people would wish to triple health care costs which means that this assertion is an instance of an attack.

Defenses can also be found on these Facebook pages. For example, Clinton criticized the GOP nominee in connection with his appearance on the "Access Hollywood" tape. Trump responded by explaining that "I've said and done things I regret, and the words released today on this more than a decade-old video are one of them.... I said it, it was wrong, and I apologize" (Donald Trump, Facebook, October 7). This statement enacts mortification (apology) but slips in a little minimization ("decade old") as well. Trump often criticized his Democratic opponent for using a private email server. Clinton's Facebook page defended against

Table 11.1. Functions and Topics of 2016 General Presidential Social Media.

	Functions			Topics	
	Acclaims	Attacks	Defenses	Policy	Character
Twitter					
Hillary Clinton	377 (45%)	**446 (54%)**	6 (1%)	186 (23%)	**637 (77%)**
Donald Trump	249 (44%)	**301 (54%)**	10 (2%)	214 (39%)	**336 (61%)**
Sub-Total	626 (45%)	**747 (54%)**	16 (1%)	400 (29%)	**973 (71%)**
Facebook					
Hillary Clinton	377 (48%)	**396 (51%)**	6 (1%)	186 (24%)	**587 (76%)**
Donald Trump	788 (49%)	790 (49%)	18 (1%)	590 (37%)	**988 (63%)**
Sub-Total	1165 (49%)	**1186 (50%)**	24 (1%)	766 (33%)	**1575 (67%)**
Hillary Clinton	754 (47%)	**842 (52%)**	12 (1%)	372 (23%)	**1224 (77%)**
Donald Trump	1037 (48%)	**1091 (51%)**	28 (1%)	804 (38%)	**1324 (62%)**
Grand Total	1791 (48%)	**1933 (51%)**	40 (1%)	1176 (32%)	**2548 (68%)**

Total Acclaims vs. Attacks: χ^2 (df = 1) = 5.41, $p < .05$
Total Topics: χ^2 (df = 1) = 505.74, $p < .0001$

this attack by observing that the "The emails weren't even on her server" (Hillary Clinton, Facebook, October 30). The second hypothesis was not confirmed. Character (68%) was in fact discussed over twice as much as policy (32%) in these posts. This contrast was statistically significant but again in the wrong direction (χ^2 [df = 1] = 505.74, $p < .0001$). The Democratic nominee discussed wages and discrimination, clearly addressing policy topics: "As president, I'll fight to pass the Paycheck Fairness Act to provide women the tools they need to fight wage discrimination" (Hillary Clinton, November 1). Trump declared that he will "MAKE AMERICA SAFE & GREAT AGAIN!" (Donald Trump, Facebook, November 2). Although Trump's utterance is more general than Clinton's; national security and prosperity also illustrate policy. Character was frequently addressed in these Facebook posts. Trump attacked Clinton's ethics and character by noting that "Crooked Hillary… deleted 33,000 emails AFTER getting a subpoena from U.S. Congress. RIGGED" (Donald Trump, Facebook, November 1). These deletions did not occur in office (i.e., as Senator or Secretary of State) but as a private person, so this attack concerns character. Clinton criticized the business magnate's leadership ability when she posted this comment: Trump "is uniquely unqualified" to be president (Hillary Clinton, November 4). These data are also reported in Table 11.1.

The first research question addressed the three forms of policy. In this sample of texts 35% concerned past deeds, 7% were about future plans, and 58% addressed

Table 11.2. Forms of Policy in 2016 General Presidential Social Media.

	Past Deeds		Future Plans		General Goals	
Twitter						
Clinton	19	10	20	19	77	41
	29 (16%)		39 (21%)		118 (63%)	
Trump	2	81	3	2	107	19
	83 (39%)		5 (2%)		126 (59%)	
Total	21	91	23	21	184	60
	112 (28%)		44 (11%)		244 (61%)	
Facebook						
Clinton	34	37	23	12	92	31
	71 (31%)		35 (15%)		123 (54%)	
Trump	2	141	2	1	361	83
	143 (24%)		3 (1%)		444 (75%)	
Sub-Total	36	178	25	13	453	114
	214 (26%)		38 (5%)		567 (69%)	
Grand Total						
Clinton	217	47	43	40	169	72
	264 (45%)		83 (14%)		241 (41%)	
Trump	4	222	5	3	468	102
	226 (28%)		8 (1%)		570 (71%)	
Total	221	269	48	43	637	174
	490 (35%)		91 (7%)		811 (58%)	

Forms of Policy: χ^2 (df = 2) = 560.81, $p < .0001$
Functions of General Goals: χ^2 (df = 1) = 264.33, $p < .0001$

general goals. This distribution was statistically significant (χ^2 [df = 2] = 560.81, $p < .0001$). Statistical analysis revealed that general goals were used more frequently as the basis for acclaims than attacks (χ^2 [df = 1] = 264.33, $p < .0001$), confirming the third hypothesis. See Table 11.2 for these data.

RQ2 concerned the relative frequency of the three forms of character. On these Facebook pages, personal qualities were most common (66%), leadership ability was the least common (7%), with the frequency of ideals falling in the middle (28%). This distribution was statistically significant (χ^2 [df = 2] = 1337.16, $p < .0001$). H4 predicted that acclaims would be based more often on ideals, compared with attacks (χ^2 [df = 1] = 263.52. $p < .0001$). These data can be found in Table 11.3.

Table 11.3. Forms of Character in 2016 General Presidential Social Media.

	Personal Qualities		Leadership Ability		Ideals	
Twitter						
Clinton	173	273	27	48	61	55
	446 (70%)		75 (12%)		116 (18%)	
Trump	108	174	12	17	17	8
	283 (84%)		29 (8%)		25 (7%)	
Total	281	447	39	65	78	63
	728 (75%)		104 (11%)		141 (14%)	
Facebook						
Clinton	44	53	9	5	62	28
	97 (48%)		14 (7%)		90 (45%)	
Trump	282	515	30	13	111	37
	797 (81%)		43 (4%)		148 (15%)	
Total	326	568	39	18	173	65
	894 (75%)		57 (5%)		238 (20%)	
Grand Total						
Clinton	217	326	36	53	123	83
	543 (65%)		89 (11%)		206 (25%)	
Trump	390	689	42	30	128	45
	1079 (81%)		72 (5%)		173 (13%)	
Total	607	1015	78	83	551	128
	1622 (66%)		161 (7%)		679 (28%)	

Forms of Character: χ^2 $(df = 2) = 1337.16, p < .0001$
Functions of Ideals: χ^2 $(df = 1) = 263.52. p < .0001$

Discussion and Conclusions

Two of the hypotheses tested here were confirmed (more acclaims than attacks on general goals and ideals) whereas two other results were not confirmed (more acclaims than attacks, more policy than character). Recall that investigation of the general presidential Facebook pages of 2012 confirmed all four of these predictions. Are the results reported here a "new normal" or are they anomalous?

Because so little research has investigated presidential candidates' use social media from the Functional perspective, we can look at research on non-presidential candidates' (senate, house, and governor) use of social media. Benoit and Stein (2018) applied Functional Theory to non-presidential candidates' use of Twitter in 2016. Tweets for all three offices used acclaims more often than attacks (and defenses least often). However, only gubernatorial tweets stressed policy over character; both Senate and House tweets emphasized character over policy. They also found that acclaims were more common, and attacks less common, when candidates for all three offices discussed general goals and ideals.

So, based on comparisons with studies on presidential candidates' use of Facebook (in 2012) and non-presidential candidates use of Twitter (in 2016), suggests that the prominence of attacks or of character could be anomalous. Only further research on the nature of social media in other campaigns should help settle these two questions.

It is possible that as social media mature their characteristics will change, so perhaps Twitter and Facebook will become more negative and mostly about policy. Benoit (2000) investigated candidate webpages in 1998 when they were a relatively new campaign medium. He found that these messages resembled resumes for the candidates and stressed character over policy. However, later work on presidential candidate webpages in 2000 (Benoit, McHale, Hansen, Pier, McGuire, 2003), 2004 (Benoit, Stein, McHale, Chattopadhyay, Verser, & Price 2007), and 2008 (Benoit, Glantz, & Rill, 2016) found that these messages emphasized policy much more than character. It is possible that social media will follow this pattern and acclaims and policy will become more prominent.

This emphasis on attacks could also be a function of the nature of the presidential candidates in 2016. Recall that Functional Theory does not declare that candidates *must* acclaim more than they attack, as they usually do. Individual candidates can, and occasionally do, stray outside the norms. Perhaps Clinton and Trump are negative people who insult and attack regularly. It is possible that they disliked each other so much they could not help attack one another. Perhaps these candidates' perceptions of the tenor of voters shifted between 2012 and 2016 so the attacks and stress on character are a result of these candidates' views of voters.

It is possible that as social media, Twitter and Facebook will tend to emphasize the candidates' character. Results from presidential candidates' use of Twitter and Facebook in 2016, as well as candidates for the Senate and House in the same year, are consistent with this possibility. Again, only time and further research will tell.

CHAPTER TWELVE

Conclusions and Comparisons

First, we review the first four hypotheses and the first three research questions. Then, this chapter will test four additional hypotheses and answer additional three research questions, with data from each of the chapters and with comparable data from previous elections. This should add to our understanding of political campaign messages generally and the 2016 presidential campaign messages specifically.

Functions of Presidential Campaign Messages

The first hypothesis predicted that acclaims would be the most common function, followed by attacks, and least frequent of all, defenses. Functional Theory and prior research support this hypothesis (Benoit, 2007, 2014a, 2014b, 2017a). This hypothesis was confirmed in all media except general TV spots, general debates, and general social media. These messages all involve Hillary Clinton and Donald Trump. It is not clear why three of their four datasets stress attacks. It could signal a shift in presidential campaign messages or it could be an idiosyncratic effect limited to these two candidates. Benoit (2015) observes that one predictor of attacks in TV spots is attacks from one's opponents. Hence, if either Clinton or Trump began the general election campaign with higher levels of attacks, the other is likely to respond in kind. Further research on future campaigns can resolve the question of whether general elections have become substantially more negative. Recall that Abramowiwts and Webster (2016, 2018) show that most voters dislike the opposing party more than they like their own party, which may encourage more attacks than in earlier years.

Target of Attacks in Presidential Primary Campaigns

The first research question concerned target of attack in primary campaign messages. Three of the five media studied stressed attacks on the other political party (announcement speeches, primary TV spots, and primary social media) but two focused most attacks on other members of the same political party (primary debates and primary TV talk shows). It is possible that no reason exists to emphasize one topic over the other.

Topic of Presidential Campaign Messages

The second prediction held that presidential campaign messages will discuss policy more than character (Benoit, 2007, 2014a, 2014b, 2017a). This hypothesis was confirmed in six message forms, all but primary social media, primary TV talk shows, and general TV spots. It is not clear why this pattern emerged. As observed earlier, Donald Trump had no prior elected experience. This limited Clinton's ability to attack on the Republican's past deeds. However, this does not explain why six media stressed policy more than character. It could be an early signal of an increased emphasis on character or it could be idiosyncratic effect.

Relative Frequency of the Forms of Policy

Research question two investigated the relative frequency of the three forms of policy. Future plans was the least common form of policy in each media. Seven of the nine media used general goals more often than past deeds (primary TV talk shows and acceptance addresses discussed past deeds most often). General goals are easy to articulate: I will create jobs or reduce illegal immigration or keep America safe from terrorists, which explains why they dominate policy discussion to the extent they do. Future plans (means) are more specific and require more time and effort to devise, which accounts for the relative infrequency of this form of policy. No prediction was advanced on the forms of policy; in the future it might make sense to predict that general goals are likely to be the most common form of policy.

Functions of General Goals

Hypothesis three held that political candidates will use general goals more to acclaim than to attack. Theory and research supports this prediction (Benoit, 2007, 2014a, 2014b, 2017a). The results of all nine message forms are in the expected direction and are significant in eight of the nine message forms.

Relative Frequency of the Forms of Character

The third research question investigated the relative frequency of the three forms of character. In eight of the nine media, personal qualities were the most common form of policy (announcement speeches stressed ideals more than personal qualities). Discussing leadership ability requires experience in elective office, which one of the two leading candidates lacked. Personal qualities, such as honesty or compassion, are usually more common than ideals such as freedom or justice. Candidates may spend less time discussing the more abstract concept of ideals.

Functions of Ideals

The fourth prediction expected that ideals would be used more often for acclaims than attacks, a hypothesis supported by both theory and past research (Benoit, 2007, 2014a, 2014b, 2017b). This prediction was upheld in every medium.

Functions of Different Sources of Campaign Message

This prediction anticipated that campaign messages from candidates would have more acclaims, and fewer attacks, than messages from other sources. TV spots in both the primary and general election phases confirmed this prediction. Presumably the assumption here is that because voters report that they dislike mudslinging (and may visit backlash on attackers), it would be better for most attacks to come from other sources than from the candidates. Of course, candidates still attack, but less than the political parties or outside groups.

Social Media Emphasize Character

H6 held that social media would discuss character more (and policy less) than other media. Table 12.1 combines primary and general campaign messages to compare

Table 12.1. Topics of 2016 Presidential Campaign Messages by Medium.

	Policy	Character
Speeches	**974 (54%)**	838 (46%)
TV Spots	**883 (56%)**	696 (44%)
Debates	**6103 (66%)**	3103 (34%)
Social Media	3484 (28%)	**8901 (72%)**
TV Talk Shows	744 (44%)	**932 (56%)**

χ^2 ($df = 4$) = 3240.8, $p < .0001$, $\varphi = .35$; Social Media vs. TV Talk Shows: χ^2 ($df = 1$) = 185.63, $p < .0001$, $\varphi = .11$

medium (remember that we could not find TV talk show texts to analyze from the general campaign). Character accounts for 72% of the utterances in social media; in contrast, character ranges from 34% to 46% in other media (character is 56% of primary TV talk shows). Statistical analysis confirms a significant difference here (χ^2 [$df = 5$] = 3240.8, $p < .0001$, $\varphi = .35$). If we compare social media vs. TV talk shows, the former stressed character more than the latter (χ^2 [$df = 1$] = 185.63, $p < .0001$, $\varphi = .11$). These data are consistent with the idea that social media are a more personal medium than speeches, spots, or debates, which suggests a greater emphasis on character than other media. Hypothesis five was confirmed in this sample. They also indicate that TV talk shows are also a more personal medium, albeit not as much as social media.

Defenses Dominate Debates

The seventh hypothesis predicts that defenses would be more common in debates than in other media. Table 12.2 again combines the data from both phases of the campaign to emphasize media. In the 2016 presidential campaign 8% of the comments in debates were defenses. In contrast, between 0.2% and 1% of the statements in other media were defenses. This contrast is statistically significant (χ^2 [$df = 6$] = 966.14, $p < .0001$, $\varphi = .14$), confirming hypothesis six. Functional Theory explains that candidates have three reasons to eschew defenses: defending may create the impression that a candidate is reactive rather than proactive, a defense likely takes a candidate off-message, and identifying an attack prior to refuting it could remind or inform voters of a potential weakness. However, the third reason does not apply to debates because the attack occurs *in the debate* and *just prior to the defense* rather than in another message or at an earlier time. Furthermore, most

Table 12.2. Frequency of Defenses in 2016 Presidential Campaign Messages.

	Acclaims	Attacks	Defenses
Speeches	1262 (69%)	559 (31%)	5 (0.3%)
TV Spots	1152 (72%)	455 (28%)	4 (0.2%)
Debates	5786 (56%)	3693 (36%)	**823 (8%)**
Social Media	6828 (61%)	4269 (38%)	112 (1%)

χ^2 (df = 6) = 966.14, p < .0001, φ = .14

candidates prepare carefully for debates, but they are not allowed to take notes in with them (and there is no teleprompter in a debate). Thus, it is possible that another reason for the relatively high frequency of defenses in debates is that candidates cannot resist responding to their opponents' taunts.

Functions of Primary versus General Campaign Messages

The Hypothesis eight predicted that acclaims would be more common, and attacks less common, in the primary campaign rather than the general campaign. Although the distribution was fairly close (62% acclaims in the primary, 60% in the general; 34% attacks in the primary, 36% in the general [plus a few defenses]), a statistically significant difference occurred in these data (χ^2 [df = 2] = 396.02, p < .0001, φ = .12). So, H8 was confirmed in these data, which are displayed in Table 12.3.

Topics of Primary versus General Campaign Messages

Hypothesis 9 expected that primary campaign messages would address policy less, and character more, than general election messages. This prediction was not upheld; in fact, the data are statistically significant in the opposite direction: primary 56% policy, 44% character; general 46% policy, 54% character (χ^2 [df = 1] = 1647.65, p < .0001, φ = .25). Hypothesis eight must be rejected based on this sample of presidential campaign messages. These results are also reported in Table 12.3.

Table 12.3. Functions of 2016 Presidential Campaign Messages.

	Functions			Topics	
	Acclaims	Attacks	Defenses	Policy	Character
Primary					
Announcements	**1023 (71%)**	406 (28%)	3 (0.2%)	**765 (54%)**	664 (46%)
TV Spots	**1016 (77%)**	295 (22%)	4 (0.3%)	**787 (60%)**	524 (40%)
Debates	**5282 (58%)**	3106 (34%)	665 (7%)	**5518 (68%)**	2636 (32%)
Social Media	**5037 (68%)**	2336 (31%)	72 (1%)	2319 (39%)	**3681 (61%)**
Total Primary	**12358 (64%)**	6143 (32%)	744 (4%)	**9389 (56%)**	7505 (44%)
General					
Acceptances	**239 (61%)**	153 (39%)	2 (0.5%)	**209 (55%)**	174 (45%)
TV Spots	136 (46%)	**160 (54%)**	0	96 (36%)	**172 (64%)**
Debates	504 (40%)	**587 (47%)**	158 (13%)	**585 (56%)**	467 (44%)
Social Media	1791 (48%)	**1933 (51%)**	40 (1%)	1166 (18%)	**5220 (82%)**
Total General	2670 (47%)	**2833 (50%)**	200 (4%)	2056 (25%)	**6033 (75%)**
Grand Total	**15028 (60%)**	8952 (36%)	944 (4%)	11445 (46%)	**13538 (54%)**

Functions of 2016 Messages versus Earlier Campaign Messages

This research question investigated here contrasted the functions (acclaims vs. attacks) and topics of 2016 presidential messages with earlier messages: announcements, primary TV spots, primary debates, primary Facebook pages (no comparable historic data are available for Twitter), acceptances, general TV spots, general debates, and general Facebook pages. We found less consistency in our analyses of primary message forms than general message forms. More attacks occurred in 2016 than earlier campaigns in announcement speeches and primary debates; fewer attacks occurred in 2016 than earlier campaigns for TV spots and Facebook pages. In 2016 primary messages, character was discussed more than policy in debates and Facebook pages; policy was addressed more in announcement speeches and TV spots.

In sharp contrast, when considering only the general election messages, the candidates attacked more than earlier messages in all four message forms investigated here: acceptances, TV spots, debates, and Facebook pages. There is no question that, based on this sample of messages, the 2016 presidential campaign was significantly more negative than earlier ones. Turning to the topics of these messages, 2016 campaign messages discussed character more, and policy less, than earlier general TV spots, debates, and Facebook pages. No difference from past campaign messages occurred in their acceptance addresses. Although

Table 12.4. Functions of 2016 versus Previous Presidential Campaign Messages.

	Functions			Topics	
	Acclaims	Attacks	Defenses	Policy	Character
Primary					
Announcements	1023 (71%)	**406 (28%)**	3 (0.2%)	**765 (54%)**	664 (46%)
1960–2012	**5122 (77%)**	1509 (23%)	19 (0.3%)	3458 (52%)	**3177 (48%)**
TV Spots	**1016 (77%)**	295 (22%)	4 (0.3%)	**787 (60%)**	524 (40%)
1952–2012	5734 (72%)	**2218 (28%)**	58 (1%)	4342 (54%)	**3626 (46%)**
Debates	5282 (58%)	**3106 (34%)**	665 (7%)	5518 (68%)	**2636 (32%)**
1948, 1960, 1968–2012	**21901 (66%)**	9666 (29%)	1667 (5%)	**21832 (70%)**	9468 (30%)
Facebook	**1162 (73%)**	416 (26%)	16 (1%)	569 (36%)	**1009 (64%)**
2012	509 (62%)	**306 (37%)**	9 (1%)	**634 (78%)**	184 (22%)
General					
Acceptances	239 (61%)	**153 (39%)**	2 (0.5%)	**209 (55%)**	174 (45%)
1952–2012	**2655 (76%)**	821 (23%)	23 (0.6%)	1887 (54%)	**1586 (46%)**
TV Spots	136 (46%)	**160 (54%)**	0	96 (36%)	**172 (64%)**
1952–2012	**3851 (54%)**	3174 (45%)	87 (1%)	**4342 (62%)**	2702 (38%)
Debates	504 (40%)	**587 (47%)**	158 (13%)	585 (56%)	**467 (44%)**
1960, 1976–2012	**4800 (57%)**	2958 (35%)	655 (8%)	**5180 (74%)**	1828 (26%)
Facebook	1165 (49%)	**1186 (50%)**	24 (1%)	766 (33%)	**1575 (67%)**
2012	**667 (59%)**	448 (40%)	13 (1%)	**839 (75%)**	276 (25%)

this conclusion is less firm than the previous one, it appears as if general election messages from 2016 stressed character more than policy. See Table 12.4 for these data.

Historic announcement data from Benoit and Glantz (2013); acceptance data from Benoit, (2014b); TV spot data from Benoit (2014a); debate data from Benoit (2014c). 2012 Facebook data are from Shen and Benoit (2016) who do not break down these posts by campaign phase. However, they report data by month and Romney clinched the Republican nomination at the end of May. Accordingly we created subtotals for 2016 Facebook data for primary (January–May) and general (July–November) campaign phases.

Acclaims vs. attacks:

Announcements: χ^2 $(df = 1) = 20.75, p < .0001, \varphi = .05$
Primary TV Spots: χ^2 $(df = 1) = 16.54, p < .0001, \varphi = .04$
Primary Debates: χ^2 $(df = 1) = 125.15, p < .0001, \varphi = .06$
Primary Facebook: χ^2 $(df = 1) = 31.9, p < .0001, \varphi = .12$

Acceptances: χ^2 (df = 1) = 44.41, $p < .0001$, $\varphi = .11$
General TV Spots: χ^2 (df = 1) = 9.2, $p < .005$, $\varphi = .04$
General Debates: χ^2 (df = 1) = 97.88, $p < .0001$, $\varphi = .11$
General Facebook: χ^2 (df = 1) = 32, $p < .0001$, $\varphi = .1$

Policy vs. Character

Announcements: χ^2 (df = 1) = .95, *ns*
Primary TV Spots: χ^2 (df = 1) = 2.25, *ns*
Primary Debates: χ^2 (df = 1) = 13.14, $p < .0005$, $\varphi = .02$
Primary Facebook: χ^2 (df = 1) = 370.21, $p < .0001$, $\varphi = .39$
Acceptances: χ^2 (df = 1) = .01, *ns*
General TV Spots: χ^2 (df = 1) = 72.15, $p < .0001$, $\varphi = .1$
General Debates: χ^2 (df = 1) = 150.52, $p < .0001$, $\varphi = .14$
General Facebook: χ^2 (df = 1) = 549.12, $p < .0001$, $\varphi = .4$

We believe that the greater consistency in general than primary campaign messages is due at least in part to the fact that primary messages were produced by many contenders (17 candidate announcement speeches, 18 TV spot sponsors, 16 debate participants, and 10 candidate's Facebook pages), whereas only two major party candidates (Clinton and Trump) are represented in our sample of general election messages.

The 2016 presidential campaign was unusually negative (e.g., Trump used name-calling). This could mean that presidential campaign discourse is becoming more negative or it is possible that these candidates are simply more nasty than earlier candidates. Note that research on political TV spots shows that candidates who are attacked are prone to respond to their opponent in kind (Walter & Nai, 2015). So, if one candidate started attacking, the other might well follow suit.

Although the evidence was not quite as clear for topic of discourse, generally the general election messages stressed character more, and policy less, than earlier general presidential campaign messages. As noted earlier, Donald Trump had no record in office to attack. In our opinion, he presented fewer (and less detailed) policy proposals than most candidates. This means the Republican could not acclaim on policy, and the Democrat could not attack on policy, as much as in previous elections.

Distribution of Forms of Policy

The second research question concerned the distribution of the three forms of policy. Functional Theory has not yet made predictions about this idea. It does suggest that general goals are easier to use than future plans: Because plans by definition

Table 12.5. Forms of Policy and Character in 2016 Campaign Messages.

Forms of Policy	Past Deeds	Future Plans	General Goals
Announcements	305 (39%)	*20 (3%)*	**450 (58%)**
Primary TV Spots	330 (42%)	*49 (6%)*	**408 (52%)**
Primary Debates	1949 (35%)	*468 (8%)*	**2122 (56%)**
Primary Social Media	819 (34%)	*60 (2%)*	**1534 (64%)**
Acceptances	86 (41%)	*7 (3%)*	**116 (56%)**
General TV Spots	31 (32%)	*7 (7%)*	**58 (60%)**
General Debates	222 (38%)	*58 (10%)*	**305 (52%)**
General Social Media	490 (35%)	*91 (7%)*	**811 (58%)**
Forms of Character	Personal Qualities	Leadership Ability	Ideals
Announcements	1181 (36%)	*573 (17%)*	**1549 (47%)**
Primary TV Spots	**274 (52%)**	*91 (17%)*	157 (30%)
Primary Debates	**1495 (55%)**	747 (27%)	*487 (18%)*
Primary Social Media	**2045 (58%)**	*604 (17%)*	886 (25%)
Acceptances	**93 (53%)**	41 (24%)	*40 (23%)*
General TV Spots	**131 (64%)**	43 (21%)	*31 (15%)*
General Debates	**329 (70%)**	203 (22%)	*35 (7%)*
General Social Media	**1622 (66%)**	*161 (7%)*	679 (28%)

The value for the most common form is set in bold; the value for the least common form is set in italics.

have details, they take longer to develop. Furthermore, some details may alienate part of the audience. A goal to reduce the national deficit is likely to be received favorably by many (if not most) voters. When one becomes more specific—reducing the deficit by raising taxes, or by cutting programs—fewer people will support the plan. These data are displayed in Table 12.5.

The distribution of the three forms of policy was quite consistent. In all eight message forms, general goals was the most common form of policy whereas future plan was the least common form of policy. Themes addressing past deeds were in the middle. The distribution of general goals and future plans was consistent with the explanation posited above (general goals are likely to be acceptable to more people that future plans).

Distribution of Forms of Character

The distribution of the three forms of character is less straightforward. Personal qualities is the most common form of character in each message form but announcement speeches. The remaining message forms are divided into two groups. In primary announcement speeches, TV spots, primary social media, and general social media, leadership ability is the least common function (and ideals are the second most common form of character [ideals with the most common form in accouncements]). In primary debates, acceptances, general TV spots, and general debates ideals are the least common function (and leadership ability is the second most common form). These data are also displayed in Table 12.5.

It may be that personal qualities are seen as the most appealing (or repellant, in attacks) form of character. Voters want presidents to be truthful (although President Trump is challenging this idea), courageous, determined, caring, and so forth; voters do not want presidents who are liars, wishy-washy, aloof, weak, and so forth. Everyone has character traits. However, leadership ability—or evidence thereof—is not something every candidate has. For example, in 2016 Trump, Carson, and Fiorina had no experience in elective office (they have other kinds of experience, but not as an elected official). They could not acclaim, or be attacked for, their experience in office, as senators and governors could. And because Obama could not run a third time and Biden decided not to seek the Oval Office, no one had experience in the office being sought. These factors could limit the discussion of leadership ability. Finally, it is possible that ideals are not prominent because they may appear ethereal rather than concrete.

Conclusion

This chapter investigates several ideas about the 2016 presidential campaign. Social media—primary and general—stress character more than other message forms. Defenses occur most frequently in debates (although in these data they were still always the least common function). Primary messages tend to be more positive than general messages. Primary messages stress character more, and policy less, than general messages. It also took up the distribution of the three forms of policy and the three forms of character. These ideas contribute to our understanding of presidential campaign messages.

There is no question that Donald Trump changed the nature of presidential campaigns. He frequently used name calling. More importantly, he relied less on television spots and more on social media. We will have to wait for future campaigns to see how much others imitate him, but his success is hard to deny. Even considering the fact that he lost the popular vote by almost three million votes, he enjoyed more success than pundits thought possible. Surely other candidates will follow in his footsteps.

APPENDIX

Meta-Analysis of Research on the Functional Theory of Political Campaign Discourse

Introduction

Election campaign messages undergird the political systems of many countries around the globe. Campaigns work to persuade citizens to cast their votes for the candidate. Legitimate criticisms can be leveled against election campaigns (e.g., candidates can be deceptive; campaign donations can corrode the process of democracy, and too many voters are apathetic), but election campaigns are ubiquitous today. In the United States candidates run for a diverse group of elective offices, including mayor, city council, congress (state and federal), governor, president, and in some jurisdictions, judgeships. The federal government in America has 537 offices (president, vice president, senators, representatives). Citizens cast votes for 18,749 positions in state government. Local (city, county) governments in the U.S. hold elections for another 500,396 elected officials. So, the United States holds elections for almost 520,000 offices (Lawless, 2012). For better or worse, the American approach to elections (use of advertising, debates, and other messages) has been used in many countries around the world. For example, political leaders' (president, prime minister, chancellor) debates have been held in many countries, including Australia, Canada, Finland, France, Germany, Ghana, Iran, Ireland, Israel, Italy, Nigeria, Northern Ireland, Poland, Scotland, South Korea, Spain, Taiwan, the Ukraine, the United Kingdom, and Wales. The use of television advertisements, however, is limited by law in some countries. Some countries limit the time period in which TV spots can be used (Kaid & Holtz-Bacha, 2006). In the UK political candidates are prohibited from running television spots. Political parties are allowed to air Party Election Broadcasts but "the maximum length of [PEBs] has declined progressively, from 30 minutes in 1955 to four minutes 40 seconds" (Scammell & Langer, 2006, p. 76). Still, TV spots are employed in many countries in contemporary election campaigns. The sheer number of campaigns is a reason for election research.

Second, literally billions of dollars are lavished on political campaigns (Benoit, 2014a). For example, Wilson (2012) determined that in the 2012 American general election presidential campaign, over a billion dollars was spent by Obama, Romney, and political groups (about twice as much as was spent in 2008). The *Washington Post* reported that as of October 19, 2016 over $3.8 billion had been raised for Democrats and Republicans in the presidential primary and general election (2016); of course, millions more were raised for down-ballot races. Additional money is spent for the hundreds of thousands of other campaigns for other political offices in the U.S. and around the world.

Third, it made a difference, for example, whether Democrat Hillary Clinton or Republican Donald Trump was elected as president in 2016. Regardless of which candidate one preferred, there is no doubt that these two candidates would pursue markedly different policies if elected. The same thing could be said of other candidates, such as Barack Obama and Mitt Romney in 2012.

Fourth, research documents effects from watching television advertising, an important campaign medium. Mulder (1979) reported that advertising in a Chicago mayoral race was positively related to attitudes toward the candidates. McClure and Patterson (1974) indicated that in the 1972 presidential campaign, "exposure to political advertising was consistently related to voter belief change" (p. 16; see also Atkin & Heald, 1976). Other research has found a positive relationship between ad spending and election outcomes (Joslyn, 1981; Palda, 1973; Wanat, 1974). Experimental research employing TV spots used by candidates in elections (Atkin, 1977; Basil, Schooler, & Reeves, 1991; Christ, Thorson, & Caywood, 1994; Faber & Storey, 1984; Faber, Tims, & Schmitt, 1993; Garramone, 1984, 1985; Garramone & Smith, 1984; Geiger & Reeves, 1991; Hitchon & Chang, 1995;` Johnston, 1989; Just, Crigler, & Wallach, 1990; Kaid, 1997; Kaid & Boydston, 1987; Kaid, Leland, & Whitney, 1992; Kaid & Sanders, 1978; Lang, 1991; McClure & Patterson, 1974; Merritt, 1984; Newhagen & Reeves, 1991) as well as studies on ads created by researchers (Becker & Doolittle, 1975; Cundy, 1986; Donohue, 1973; Garramone, Atkin, Pinkleton, & Cole, 1990; Hill, 1989; Meadow & Sigelman, 1982; Roddy & Garramone, 1988; Rudd, 1989; Thorson, Christ, & Caywood, 1991) demonstrates that televised political advertisements have a variety of effects (recall of ad content, attitudes toward candidates, voting intention) on viewers. Based on the 2000 and 2004 presidential elections, Gordon and Hartmann (2013) reported that "our findings illustrate that advertising is capable of shifting the electoral votes of multiple states and consequently the outcome of an election" (p. 33). Significant effects from TV spots have been confirmed through meta-analysis (Benoit, Leshner, & Chattopadhyay, 2007). Campaign messages do not affect every citizen, and they do not influence every one in the same way (Jarman, 2005), but they inform a significant number of voters and change or reinforce existing attitudes for many.

Research has established that debates—another important campaign medium—have several effects on those who watch them (see, e.g., Benoit, Hansen, & Holbert, 2004; Benoit, McKinney, & Holbert, 2001; Benoit, McKinney, & Stephenson, 2002; Benoit & Stephenson, 2004; Benoit, Webber, & Berman, 1998; Holbrook, 1996; McKinney & Carlin, 2004; Racine Group, 2002; Reinemann & Maurer, 2005; Shaw, 1999a, 1999b). Patterson (2003) reported that "Citizens learn more about the candidates during the ninety minutes of an October debate than they do in most other weeks of the campaign" (pp. 170–171). Significant effects from watching debates have been confirmed through meta-analysis (Benoit, Hansen, & Verser, 2003). Research confirms effects of watching debates in non-presidential campaigns (e.g., Just, Crigler, & Wallach, 1990) and non-U.S. campaign debates (e.g., Blumler, 2011; Senior, 2008).

Sides and Vavreck (2013) offered a useful metaphor for understanding campaign effects, comparing presidential election campaigns to "a game of tug-of-way. Both sides are pulling very hard. If for some reason, one side let go—meaning they stop campaigning—the other side would soon benefit" (p. 9). So, if either major candidate in a contested election ceased producing campaign messages he or she would quickly drop in the polls. Campaign effects may not always be obvious but messages have substantial effects and can be very important.

Campaigns enable candidates to connect with citizens and provide opportunities for voters to participate in democracy. The candidate election messages that constitute campaigns deserve scholarly attention. Textual literature reviews of research on Functional Theory are available in Benoit (2007, 2014a, 2014c). The purpose of this study is to report meta-analyses of data on ten Functional Theory predictions.

Meta-analysis (see, e.g., Glass, McGaw, & Smith, 1981; Hunter & Schmidt, 1990, 2004; Rosenthal, 1991; or Wolf, 1986) is a statistical method for cumulating the findings of multiple studies of a given dependent variable. This method has important advantages over traditional, narrative literature reviews. First, it works from effect size rather than significance levels; significance levels are highly dependent on sample size. Second, meta-analysis provides a statistical (relatively objective) approach to summarizing past research. Furthermore, it permits corrections for such factors as sampling error and measurement error.

Functional Theory of Political Campaign Discourse

Functional Theory was developed for several reasons. First, far too much research into the nature (content) of election campaign messages is atheoretical. Functional Theory articulates assumptions about election discourse and offers several predictions about the content of such messages. Second, content analysis of political TV spots is quite common in the literature (with most research analyzing functions—positive versus negative ads—and/or topic—issue versus image ads). However, comparatively little research investigated the nature of other kinds of election messages, such as announcement speeches, televised primary and general election debates, announcement speeches and acceptance addresses, or candidate webpages. Functional Theory proposes a method that can be, and has been, applied across campaign media (and across level of office and country). Third, the content analysis that has been conducted of advertisements had limitations. Some studies do not examine both functions and topics (Functional Theory analyzes both topics). Most research uses the entire spot as the coding unit: TV spots were coded either as positive or negative (a few studies added a third possibility, comparative ads) and coded as addressing either policy or character. Kaid and Johnston (1991) acknowledged that using the entire spot as a coding unit has potential limitations: "Our method of dichotomizing the sample into positive and negative ads by determining a dominant focus on the candidate or his opponent is useful for analysis but may understate the amount of negative information about an opponent present even in a positive ad" (p. 62). Coding entire spots could also lead researchers to overestimate attacks. To illustrate this potential problem, consider this spot for George W. Bush in 2000:

> **Announcer:** *Under Clinton/Gore, prescription drug prices have skyrocketed, and nothing's been done.* George Bush has a plan: Add a prescription drug benefit to Medicare.
>
> **Bush:** Every senior will have access to prescription drug benefits.
>
> **Announcer:** *And Al Gore? He says he wants to fight for the people against HMOs, but his prescription drug plan forces seniors into one HMO selected by the federal government. Al Gore: Federal HMO.* George Bush: Seniors choose.

Italicized utterances attack Gore whereas the other remarks acclaim Bush. To describe this entire spot as *either* positive *or* negative clearly erroneously classifies part of what is being said to voters. Even classifying this as a comparative ad (which implies a 50/50 split) overlooks the fact that about two-thirds of this ad is negative and one-third positive. Compare that ad, with both acclaims and attacks, with this spot used in the same campaign:

> 2.2 trillion dollars. That's a lot of money: 8,000 dollars for each American. It's our government's projected surplus over the next 10 years. Al Gore plans to spend it all and more. Gore's proposing three times the new spending President Clinton proposed, wiping out the entire surplus and creating a deficit again. Gore's big government spending plan threatens American prosperity.

Unlike the previous advertisement, this one is entirely negative. Yet using the entire ad as the coding unit would "count" these two messages the same, each as one attacking ad. The same problem arises in studies coding a spot as addressing either issue or image. Kaid (1994) took the unusual step of dividing presidential primary ads from the 1992 campaign into three groups: image ads, issue ads, and negative ads, a category system that implies that image and issue ads were distinct from negative spots. Surely negative ads can address issues and image (or both), but this classification system does not make that point clear. Benoit and Airne (2009), for example, studying Senate, House, and gubernatorial ads from 2004, found that 42% o the ads in their sample contained both acclaims and attacks and 75% of spots discussed both policy and character. Coding by themes allows the analysis to more accurately represent the content of these messages. Benoit and Benoit-Bryan (2014a) explain that "Themes are complete ideas, claims, or arguments; a single theme can vary in length from one phrase to an entire paragraph" (p. 159). A moment's reflection will reveal that using the entire message as the coding unit would be useless for content analysis of speeches or other message forms.

Fourth, much research on the content of election messages does not report inter-coder reliability (e.g., Ridout & Holland, 2010). Other research reports inter-coder reliability as simple agreement between coders. With two categories (positive or negative; issue or image) even monkeys pounding on a keyboard are likely to agree 50% of the time. Functional Theory uses Cohen's (1960) κ, which controls for agreement by chance. This means we can place greater confidence in data produced by the Functional Theory than in many other studies.

A fifth limitation of past research is that few studies go beyond functions (positive, negative) or topics (issue, image); Functional Theory divides the topics of policy and character into sub-categories (past deeds, future plans, general goals; personal qualities, leadership ability, ideals). Statements about policy and character can be sub-divided into more specific kinds of statements. Finally, Functional Theory ads a third function, defenses (refutations of attacks). Defenses are quite rare in political advertising, so this is not a telling criticism of research on ads, but in debates defenses can account for 5–10% of the candidate remarks. Thus, Functional Theory was developed in response to limitations of the existing literature.

Election campaign information originates from candidates, other sources (such as PACs or other politicians), and the news media. Candidates can reach voters directly (path 1) when a citizen sees a TV spot, visits a candidate's Facebook page, watches a debate, reads a candidate's tweets, and so forth. Candidates reach voters indirectly when information from a candidate's message reaches one voter directly (path 2) who then passes that information along to friends, family, or co-workers in political discussion (path 3). Candidates also send information (e.g., press releases) to the media (path 4). Other sources, such as PACs or other politicians, send information to voters directly in TV spots or other messages (path 5), to voters indirectly through political discussion (path 6 and then path 3) and to the media (path 7). The news media passes some of the information it receives from candidates and other sources to voters, often with commentary or evaluation, and news media originate some information. Information from the news media reaches some voters directly (path 8) when they watch or read the news and indirectly through political discussion (path 9 and then path 3).

This approach has received growing acceptance. For example, Nai and Walter (2015) edited a book on negative campaigning, adopting Functional Theory "as a baseline for defining and measuring negative campaigning" (p. 17). Hrbkova and Zagrapan (2014), studying political leaders' debates, wrote that "The most influential attempt at systematic analysis of political debates based on a specific theoretical construct is the functional theory by William Benoit" (p. 736). Isotalus (2011) wrote that "One of the most used and systematically tested theories in the studies of the content of television debates has been functional theory" (p. 31). This theory merits scholarly attention.

This theory makes five assumptions about election campaigns (Benoit, 2007). First, voting is a comparative act. To win elective office, candidates only need to appear—and it is important to remember that political campaigns are about voters' perceptions—preferable to their opponents. Candidates do need not to persuade all citizens (or even all voters) of their superiority; they must only persuade enough voters to win the election. The idea that political candidates do not have to persuade all voters of their preferability is very important because many issues are controversial and people disagree about the most important character traits of a president: Candidates cannot hope to persuade all voters of their preferability on either policy or character. Candidates who espouse a particular position on any given controversial issue are likely to simultaneously attract and repel different groups of voters who embrace different beliefs and values; it is lucky that a political candidate does not have to persuade all voters to win an election.

Second, candidates must call attention to areas of contrast between themselves and their opponent(s). Those seeking elective office do not have to disagree with opponents on every conceivable issue: Who would oppose curbing inflation, creating jobs, or protecting the country from terrorists? Nevertheless, voters would have no reason to prefer one candidate over another if the candidates appear identical in every regard. Candidates must distinguish themselves from opponents on at least some points of comparison if they are to appear preferable to opponents. The need to reach voters to create some contrasts between or among candidates means that communication is vital to political election campaigns.

The third assumption is that citizens obtain information about candidates and their issue stands through election messages from a variety of sources, including candidates, their supporters, the news media, and special interest groups. Candidates use messages in a variety of media to inform voters about themselves and their policies and to identify differences between opponents, including TV spots, debates, speeches, webpages, and Facebook pages.

Fourth, candidates can establish preferability to opponents by using messages that employ the functions of acclaims, attacks, and defenses. Acclaims tout a candidate's strengths or advantages. Attacks identify an opponent's alleged weaknesses or disadvantages. Defenses respond to, or refute, attacks made against a candidate. These functions work together as an informal version of cost-benefit analysis. This observation does not mean Functional Theory assumes that voters quantify benefits (acclaims) or costs (attacks and defenses) or that they engage in mathematical calculations (adding or averaging costs and benefits) to make vote choices. Acclaims are capable of increasing a candidate's perceived benefits. Attacks can increase the apparent costs of an opponent. Defenses have the potential to reduce a candidate's perceived costs. Functional Theory does not assume that acclaims, attacks, and defenses are necessarily persuasive: Some messages are poorly conceived or do not reach the intended audience; some voters are far from open-minded. Furthermore, knowledge and attitudes of voters differs, as does the way citizens perceive messages from and about candidates.

Election discourse can address two potential topics, policy and character, a fifth assumption of Functional Theory. Candidates can acclaim, attack, and defend (1) *what he or she has done or will do* in office (policy) and (2) *who he or she is* (character). These terms (policy, character) are preferable to other terms often encountered in the literature: issue and image. The term "issue" refers to disputable questions. Because candidates often discuss their personalities, it is possible for *character* to be an *issue* in a campaign. Furthermore, citizens develop perceptions—impressions or images—of the candidates' policy positions as well as their character, which means one could talk about voters' *images* of the candidates' *policy* positions. Using the terms policy and character avoids these potential difficulties.

It is important to note that these two topics are not entirely discrete. When a candidate takes a particular position on an issue (policy) could influence the audience's perceptions of that candidate (character). For example, espousing a proposal to help the homeless (policy) could foster the impression that the candidate is compassionate (character). Similarly, a candidate thought to be a bigot (a character trait) could be assumed to oppose legislation to help minorities (policy). Still, legislation to help the homeless or on minorities is different from the personal qualities of compassion or bigotry. High values for inter-coder reliability in research using the Functional approach (see below) on topics of campaign discourse demonstrates that despite some overlap, policy and character are distinct topics.

Functional theory further divides discourse on policy into past deeds (record in office), future plans (means or specific proposals for policy), and general goals (ends, desired future state of affairs). Functional Theory focuses on the past (past deeds) and the future (future plans and general goals). It does not have a category to represent campaign discourse using the present tense. For example, candidates sometimes make statements like "I am working hard to create jobs." If this work has actually created any jobs, that accomplishment should be (and almost certainly would be) used as the basis for an acclaim on past deeds (e.g., "Job creation increased 15% under my stewardship"). If that hard work has not actually produced any results, the statement is essentially an acclaim on general goals ("My goal is job creation"). This analysis comports well with theories of voting from political science which identify two theories of vote choice: Retrospective voting, where vote choice is based on an assessment of what the candidates have accomplished in the past, versus prospective voting, which bases vote choice on speculation about what the candidates will likely accomplish (in the future) if elected (Lanoue, 1994). There is no third theory of voting concerned with the present. Functional Theory also sub-divides utterances on character into statements about personal qualities (personality), leadership ability (experience in elective office, ability to lead), and ideals (values or principles, this concept is not derived from social psychology). Figure 1 illustrates the basic concepts of Functional Theory by providing hypothetical examples to illustrate acclaims, attacks, and defenses on the three forms of policy and of character.

Message Content	Acclaim Self	Defend Self	Attack Opponent
Policy			
Past Deeds	I created jobs	Unemployment was caused by my predecessor	Opponent failed to fight crime
Future Plans	My proposal will destroy ISIS	My plan does not cut taxes on the rich	Opponent's tax plan will help the rich and hurt the middle class
General Goals	I want to keep America safe	I want to stop illegal immigration	Opponent wants to discriminate against Muslims
Character			
Personal Qualities	I can be trusted	I am not a liar	Opponent is immoral
Leadership Ability	I have served as Governor of a large state	As Vice President I had important responsibilities	Opponent lacks experience in running a government
Ideals	Everyone has a right to justice	I do not think people are entitled to government handouts	Opponent thinks everyone should fend for themselves

Figure 1. A Schematic Outline of Functional Theory.

Predictions

The Functional Theory of Political Campaign Discourse makes a number of predictions, 11 of which are tested here (it also offers other predictions—e.g., that news coverage discusses attacks more than candidates actually use attacks—but the data on these other predictions are too sparse to justify meta-analysis).

Acclaims have no drawbacks, attacks have one drawback (many voters dislike mudslinging, so an attack can generate backlash—see, e.g., Merritt, 1984; Stewart, 1975), and defenses have three limitations (defenses can make a candidate appear reactive rather than proactive; because attacks usually address the target's weaknesses, defenses often take a candidate off message; one must identify an attack in order to refute it, so a defense can inform or remind voters of a potential weakness). So, candidates have reasons to use more acclaims than attacks and more attacks than defenses. Some authors believe that attacks are very common in candidate messages. For example, West (2001) indicated that more of advertisements were negative than positive. Kamber (1997), for example, notes that "previous eras saw severe personal attack on political candidates, but they also saw detailed and sometimes inspiring deliberation over the issues. Our present political discourse is nothing but spleen" (p. 4). Broder (2002), a journalist, wrote that "the ads people are seeing are relentlessly negative… often never a hint as to why a voter should support the person paying for the TV spot." However, Functional Theory predicts that acclaims are more common than attacks.

> H1. Acclaims will be more common than attacks.

Concerns about backlash from attacks are only one consideration that influences the frequency of attacks in campaign messages. For example, challengers tend to attack more than incumbents, candidates who trail their opponents usually attack more than leaders, the frequency of attacks by a candidate is directly related to the number of attacks made against that candidate, the use of attacks is directly related to competitiveness, attacks increase as election day approaches, and ads sponsored by political parties and political groups are usually more negative than spots from candidates (see, e.g., Benoit, 2014a; Damore, 2002; Elmelund-Praestekaer, 2010; Maier & Jansen, 2015; Ridout & Holland, 2010; Sullivan & Sapir, 2012). Presidential television advertisements from candidates who trailed throughout the general election campaign attacked more often than their opponents (who led during the entire general election campaign) or candidates in races where the lead changed during the campaign (Benoit, 2014a).

It is important to acknowledge that attacks are not inherently false or misleading (Benoit, 2013): Some attacks are reasonable just as some acclaims are false or misleading. Geer (2006) argues that informed decision making requires an understanding of pros and cons, so attacks can be an important part of the democratic process. He also notes that attacks are more likely to include evidence than acclaims. Defenses are consistently the least common function so this function was not included in this prediction.

A second prediction holds that candidates for elective office will discuss policy more often than character. Many believe that character is more important than policy. Clarke and Evans (1983) surveyed 82 reporters, concluding that:

> Strikingly, issue-related topics recede when reporters turn to analyzing the strengths and weaknesses that they think will determine the election…. On the whole, candidates do not dwell on these [personal] characteristics in their appeals to voters. Yet journalists believe that they are important factors in determining the outcome of a congressional race. (pp. 39–42)

Skewes (2007) notes that "in covering candidates for the White House, the one aspect of coverage that journalists universally agreed was important… was coverage of the candidates' character" (p. 57). So, many writers hold the belief that character is more important than policy. Research has demonstrated that the *New York Times* reports character remarks more often than candidates make such remarks (Benoit, Hemmer, & Stein, 2010; Benoit, Stein, & Hansen, 2005). News coverage of American senate, gubernatorial, and mayoral election campaigns (Benoit, Compton, & Phillips, 2013) and of prime minister campaigns in Australia, Canada, and the United Kingdom (Benoit, Furgerson, Seifert, & Sargardia, 2013) show the same pattern, with news discussing character more than the candidates themselves. However, King (2002) noted the "almost universal belief that leaders' and candidates' personalities are almost invariably hugely important in determining the outcomes of elections is simply wrong" (p. 216). Scholars and journalists alike stress character over policy.

Of course, some citizens do think the most important function of a president (prime minister, chancellor) is to serve as a role model (character) but more voters see the most important factor in evaluating political leaders is their work proposing and implementing governmental policy. Consistent with this belief, public opinion polls in the U.S. reveals that more respondents say policy is a more important determinant for their vote for president than character (Benoit, 2003). Benoit also contrasted the topics of candidates who won (primary, acceptance, general; primary and general TV spots and debates, acceptance addresses): Winners were significantly more likely to discuss policy, and less likely to discuss character, than losers. Hofstetter (1976) explains that "issue preferences are key elements in the preferences of most, if not all, voters" (p. 77). King (2002) analyzed research on the role of character in 51 elections held in 6 countries between 1960 and 2001 confirming that "It is quite unusual for leaders' and candidates' personality and other personal traits to determine election outcomes" (p. 216). So, most voters consider policy to be more important than character in deciding their presidential vote and election results (voting patterns) are consistent with this belief.

H2. Candidates will address policy more often than character.

Baker and Norpoth's (1981) analysis of the 1972 West German debates found that candidates discussed issues more than ethics (character), consistent with this prediction. H7, discussed below, considers the influence of campaign phase on topic of campaign message.

Incumbency is another variable capable of influencing the functions of campaign discourse (see Dover, 2006, for a treatment of incumbency in presidential TV spots). Scholars have identified several advantages possessed by incumbents. For example, Salamore and Salamore (1995) state that incumbents have greater recognition, ability to raise campaign funds, and ability to begin campaigning early. Incumbents are also likely to receive even more attention from the press than challengers (see, e.g., Smith, 2005; Smith & Mansharamani, 2002; Trent & Trent, 1974, 1995). In almost all cases the incumbent will be better known than the challenger, particularly if the incumbent party candidate is an incumbent president running for re-election. This means that knowledge of, and attitudes about, candidates are likely easier to change for challengers than incumbents. Unless an incumbent is unpopular, challengers must give voters a reason to evict the incumbent and attacks are usually the basis for that argument.

> H3. Incumbents will acclaim more, and attack less, than challengers.

This contrast should be particularly sharp when the candidates discuss past deeds or record in office. Only incumbents have a record in the office sought in an election. Challengers often have records in other offices, such as governor or senator. However, experience in other elective offices is simply not comparable to experience in the White House (e.g., presidents negotiate treaties and serve as commander in chief); the incumbent's record in the Oval Office is the best evidence of how a candidate will perform in elected. As the data in Table 5 reveal, both incumbents and challengers discuss the incumbent's record in office (past deeds) more than the challenger's record: Incumbents discuss their own record in 70% of statements about past deeds and the challenger's record in 30% of themes on record in office. Challengers discuss the incumbent's record in 75% of utterances about past deeds and their own record in 25% of their statements on this topic. Obviously, when discussing their own record incumbents acclaim; when discussing the incumbent's record, challengers attack. Statistical analysis reveals this contrast is significant with a large effect size (χ^2 [df = 1] = 4153.33, $p < .0001$, $\varphi = .45$). Non-presidential campaigns without incumbents running for re-election are considered "open seat" elections and not used in the tests of H4 (or H5).

> H4. When discussing past deeds (record in office), incumbents will acclaim more, and attack less, than challengers.

So, incumbents as a group are likely to acclaim more, and attack less, than challengers—particularly when the candidates talk about past deeds.

> H5. When discussing future plans, incumbents will attack more and acclaim less than challengers.

The fifth prediction anticipates that when discussing future plans (specific policy proposals), incumbents will acclaim less and attack more than challengers. Proposing a future plan implicitly indicts the incumbent, who has failed to implement a desirable change in policy. Of course, it would be unwise for an incumbent to assert that everything is perfect and no changes are needed. But every time either candidate offers a proposal for policy change, these future plans suggest something is not going well under the incumbent. This means that challengers are more likely to acclaim on future plans than incumbents. Because more future plans are likely to be proposed by the challenger, more opportunities exist for incumbents, compared to challengers, to attack future plans.

Functional Theory anticipates that messages from the primary phase of the campaign will differ in predictable ways from general election messages (see, e.g., Davis, 1997; Kendall, 2000; Mayer, 2000; Norrander, 2000; Palmer, 1997). The primary phase pits candidates against other members of the same political party. In 2016, for example, Donald Trump contested the Republican nomination with Jeb Bush, Ben Carson, Chris Christie, Ted Cruz, Mike Huckabee, Ron Paul, Marco Rubio, and Scott Walter. Hillary Clinton ran against Lincoln Chafee, Martin O'Malley, Bernie Sanders, and Jim Webb. Of course, every differs somewhat from other members of the same party, but greater differences are likely to exist when candidates of different parties clash in the general election. Fewer policy differences among candidates means fewer opportunities to attack; more policy differences mean more opportunities to attack. Also, in the primary campaign phase candidates have an incentive to moderate their attacks. In the primary, every candidate wants the losing opponents to support him or her in the general election. So for example, if Ted Cruz had won the 2016 Republican primary, he would have wanted Ben Carson, Marco Rubio, Chris Christie, John Kasich, and the others to advocate for him during the general campaign. Even more importantly, every nominee in the general election wants the support of all party members, including those who preferred a different candidate during the primary. Both of these considerations (support from other candidates, support from other candidates' partisans) provide a reason to moderate attacks in the primary, so as not to offend other candidates or the other candidates' supporters. This constraint does not exist in the general election campaign.

H6. More attacks, and fewer acclaims, will be used in general election messages than in primary messages.

Benoit (2014a) isolated presidential candidates who won their party's nomination and who therefore deployed both primary TV spots and general ads: 21 of the 22 candidates acclaimed more, and attacked less, in their primary ads than they did in their general spots.

Another difference between primary and general elections is that generally candidates are less well-known in the primary than the general election. In 2016, for example, relatively few people knew Ben Carson and his issue positions. The same can be said for other candidates such as John Kasich, Ted Cruz, Marco Rubio and Bernie Sanders. The candidates' need to introduce themselves in the primary is a reason to stress character in that phase. Furthermore, as noted earlier, fewer policy differences exist between members of the same party (in the primary) than between nominees from different political parties. It is easier for candidates to differentiate themselves from candidates of the other party than candidates of the same political party.

> H7. General campaign messages will discuss policy more, and character less, than primary election messages.

Data comparing TV spots from primary and general campaigns confirm this prediction. When looking exclusively at presidential candidates who ran spots in both phases of the campaign, 20 of 22 candidates' ads were consistent with this prediction (Benoit, 2014a).

Functional Theory offers predictions about the forms of policy and character (in addition to the predictions about incumbency and past deeds, incumbency and future plans). It is easier to for a candidate to embrace (acclaim) general goals and ideals than to reject them (attack). For instance, what candidate would oppose reducing inflation or keeping America safe? Similarly, candidates are less likely to attack than acclaim when discussing ideals: It is difficult to criticize values and principles such as freedom, equal opportunity, or justice. This consideration leads to two hypotheses.

> H8. When discussing general goals, candidates will acclaim more than they attack.

> H9. When discussing ideals, candidates will acclaim more than they attack.

The next prediction proposed here contrasts two forms of policy: future plans (means) and general goals (ends). It is more difficult to attack general goals than future plans. For example, candidates might agree that we should reduce taxes (a goal) but disagree about how to achieve this end (across the board tax cuts or targeted reductions, and, if the latter, which programs should be targeted for reduction?). This consideration may incline candidates to be somewhat vague: The more details a candidate provides about policy, the easier it for opponents to attack.

> H10. Acclaims will be used more often to discuss general goals than future plans; attacks will be more common when candidates address future plans.

Acclaims should be more common than attacks when discussing both of these two forms of policy; however, attacks should be more difficult to make against general goals than future plans.

An important variable in the process of communication is the source. Kaid and Johnston (2001) reported that ads with speaking used fewer attacks than spots featuring anonymous announcers or surrogate speakers. Franz, Freedman, Goldstein, and Ridout (2008) found that candidate-sponsored advertisements included fewer attacks than those from Interest groups and political party ads (see also Benoit, 2014b; or Sullivan & Sapir, 2012). The idea here is that attacks can create backlash from voters who detest mudslinging. Candidates do make attacks, but they prefer to have other sources produce most of the attacks. Hopefully, if a backlash from attacks occurs with some voters, it will damage the surrogate sources more than the candidate. Accordingly, Functional Theory predicts that

H11. Candidates use more acclaims, and fewer attacks, than other sources.

It is important to note that Functional Theory's predictions are not laws but reasons. For example, it does not hold that acclaims *must* outnumber attacks, just that candidates have reasons to acclaim more than they attack. Individual candidates can choose to attack more than they acclaim. The same is true of other predictions (e.g., candidates have reasons to discuss policy more than character, but Functional Theory does not assert that they *must* do so).

Functional Theory, particularly as applied to political leaders' debates, has generated criticism. Isotalus and Aarnio (2006) argue that this theory "seems to be more appropriate for a two-party system but it is of a limited value for a multi-party system" (p. 64). However, Functional Theory has been successfully applied to political leaders' debates in several multi-party systems: Australia 2013 (Benoit & Benoit-Bryan, 2015); Canada 2006 (Benoit & Henson, 2007) and 2011 (Benoit, 2011); Northern Ireland 2010 (Benoit & Benoit-Bryan, 2014b); Scotland 2010 (Benoit & Benoit-Bryan, 2014b), South Korea 2002 (Lee & Benoit, 2005), 1997 (Choi & Benoit, 2009), and 2002 (Choi & Benoit, 2009); the United Kingdom (Benoit & Benoit-Bryan, 2013); and Wales 2010 (Benoit & Benoit-Bryan, 2014b). Some research (e.g., Dudek & Partcaz, 2009; Hrbkova & Zagrapan, 2014) provides only partial support for Functional Theory's predictions; it is possible that this inconsistency stems in part cultural differences or from other scholars' failure to use an extensive codebook, as does Functional research. This could also mean that the inconsistent data is less reliable than the data employed here.

This analysis used the correlation coefficient *r* as opposed to other measures of effect size (e.g., Cohen's *d*; see Hunter & Schmidt, 1990, 2004). Two corrections were made to the effect sizes. First, the effect sizes were corrected for measurement error by using the reliability for each variable for each study. After this step, sampling error was corrected by weighting the average overall effect size by the number of subjects in the study. Hunter and Schmidt (1990) noted that if the population correlation is assumed to be consistent across all studies then "the best estimate of that correlation is not the simple mean across studies but a weighted average in which each correlation is weighted by the number of persons in that study" (p. 100). All things being equal, studies with larger sample sizes provide a better estimate of the population parameter being measured and deserve to be weighted more than studies with smaller sample sizes.

Data

This meta-analysis employs data from many sources. Table 1 describes the sample. The data are taken from content analysis of many candidates, multiple campaigns (years), multiple media, different offices, and messages from the U.S. and other countries. The search for studies began with Loudan's (2016) bibliography of publications on election campaigns. An Internet search was conducted, using the search term "Functional Theory" combined with other terms: "debates," "television spots," "television advertising," "television commercials," "announcement speeches," "acceptance addresses," "acceptance speeches," "webpages," "brochures," "direct mail," and "pamphlets." Google Scholar was also employed to locate publications that cite Functional Theory publications (Benoit, 2007; Benoit et al., 1999, 2008; Benoit, Brazeal, & Airne, 2007; Benoit & Klyukovski, 2006; Benoit & Sheafer, 2006; Benoit & Stein, 2005; Brazeal & Benoit, 2006). Each time a pertinent publication was located, the references were examined to locate additional studies. Studies had to report the *n* and the effect size (or a statistic that could be converted into an effect size) to be included in the sample. Some studies provided data for only some of the predictions (e.g., many studies reported no data on primary campaign messages). In only one case did two studies report the same data. Benoit and Brazeal (2001) analyzed non-presidential TV spots from 1986 to 2000. Benoit and Brazeal (2006) extended that study, supplementing the sample of 1986–2000 with ads broadcast in 1980, 1982, 1984, 2002, and 2004. Because the second study includes all of the data from Benoit and Brazeal (2001) along with "new" data, only data reported in Benoit and Brazeal (2006) were included in the meta-analysis.

A few studies (e.g., Dudek & Partcaz, 2009; Hrbkova & Zagrapan, 2014; Isotalus, 2011) were not included in the sample because they did not report reliability. The effect size (*r*) from each hypothesis was corrected for measurement error (reliability) and weighted by sample size: A weighted mean effect size was calculated for each hypothesis and a confidence interval was constructed to test the significance of this weighted mean effect size.

Table 1. Sample of Messages in the Meta-Analysis.

Message Form	Years (or countries)	Number of Messages
Announcement Speeches	1960–2012	114
Primary TV Spots	1952–2012	1516
Primary Debates	1948, 1960, 1968, 1972, 1980–2012	173
Primary Brochures	1948–2004	270
Candidate Primary Webpages	2000, 2004, 2008	38
Acceptance Addresses	1952–2012	64
General TV Spots	1952–2012	1362
General Debates	1960, 1976–2012	29
Vice Presidential Debates	1976, 1984–2012	9
General Brochures	1948–2004	445
Candidate General Webpages	2000, 2004, 2008	6
Candidate General Facebook	2008, 2012	4
Gubernatorial Debates	1994–2004	15
Gubernatorial TV Spots	1974–2008	1347
Senate Debates	1998–2006	21
Senate TV Spots	1980–2008	1586
House TV Spots	1980–2008	782
Mayoral Debates	2005–2007	10
Mayoral candidate webpages	2013	13
Non-U.S. Debates	Australia, Canada, France, Germany, Israel, South Korea, Spain, Taiwan, Ukraine, UK	18

It is important to distinguish the three different *n*s reported here; one reason this is important is that significance levels are sensitive to sample size. For example, consider H1 on the functions of messages. One message form used to test H1 was primary TV spots; Table 1 reports an *n* of 1516, the number of different primary TV spots that were content analyzed in this sample. The *n* used to calculate the *r* for primary TV ads in H2 is the number of themes coded for these spots, 7952 (reported in Table 2). Combining all message forms, the total *n* of messages used to test H1 is 7911 (7911 debates, TV spots, speeches, etc.); the total *n* of themes in these studies is 181,830. These two *n*s provide a high degree of confidence in the *r*s calculated for each message form. However, the third *n*, used to calculate confidence intervals to testing the significance of H1, is the number of *message forms* (e.g., primary TV spots, primary debate), which is 15 for this hypothesis. This means that, when a significant result is reported for a meta-analysis, that

Table 2. Functions of Political Campaign Messages.

Message	Acclaims	Attacks	χ^2	*n*	Corrected *r*
Announcement Speeches	5418 (76%)	1718 (24%)	1917.4	7136	.55
Acceptance Addresses	2652 (76%)	821 (24%)	964.26	3473	.6
Primary Brochures	8207 (84%)	1526 (16%)	4586.02	9733	.73
General Brochures	8149 (71%)	3398 (29%)	1953.98	11547	.43
Primary Spots	5734 (72%)	2218 (28%)	1553.72	7952	.47
General Spots	3851 (55%)	3174 (45%)	65.04	7025	.1
Primary Debates	25428 (69%)	11231 (31%)	5497.82	36659	.43
General Debates	5519 (62%)	3332 (38%)	539.9	8851	.27
Primary Webpages	14308 (94%)	972 (6%)	11637.58	15280	.95
General Webpages	12110 (91%)	1154 (9%)	9047.96	13264	.89
Vice Presidential Debates	2912 (58%)	2137 (42%)	118.66	5049	.16
Non-Presidential Spots	15415 (70%)	6552 (30%)	3575.14	21967	.43
Non-Presidential Debates	6662 (70%)	2910 (30%)	1469.92	9572	.41
Mayoral Webpages	5628 (93%)	418 (7%)	4489.6	6046	.97
Non-U.S. Debates	10978 (60%)	7298 (40%)	740.6	18276	.22
Total *n*	weighted corrected *r*	*sd*			
181,830	.50	.28	$p < .05$		

significance is not a consequence of the large sample of spots (or other messages) or the large number of themes involved.

Because all the tests reported here concerned predictions, one-sided confidence intervals of .05 were used for significance testing. Significant effect sizes were tested for homogeneity of variance: All significant effect sizes in this meta-analysis had heterogeneous variance. This is not surprising given Functional Theory's assumption that candidates choose the content of their messages. No obvious variable accounted for heterogeneity of variance for any hypothesis.

The data reported here are highly reliable. Inter-coder reliability in these studies was calculated using Cohen's (1960) κ, which controls for agreement by chance. For example, in Benoit, McHale, Hansen, Pier, & McGuire (2003) five co-authors had κs of .79–1.0 for function, .76–.98 for topic, .91–1.0 for forms of policy, and .78–1.0 for forms of character. Benoit, Stein, McHale, Chattopadhyay, Verser, & Price (2007) with six co-authors also had high inter-coder reliability, with κs of .82–1.0 for function, .82–97 for topic, .75–1.0 for forms of policy, and .76–.92 for forms of character. Landis and Koch (1977) explain that values of *kappa* from 0.61 to 0.80 represent "substantial" agreement and values from 0.81 to 1.0 reflect "almost perfect" inter-coder reliability (p. 165). This high level of reliability may stem from the detailed codebook and coding rules developed for Functional Theory.

Validity can be difficult to establish. However, some evidence supports the validity of these data. Geer (2006) argued that his data were validated because his measure of negativity in TV spots "correlates… a staggering 0.97 with Benoit's" measure (p. 36). His data, in turn, support the validity of the data reported here.

The *r*s for each message form were corrected for measurement error using the reliability coefficient for that data. Then the corrected *r*s were weighted by sample size. The *sd* of the corrected *r*s were used to construct confidence intervals. If the confidence interval includes zero, the corrected weighted *r* was not significant. If the confidence interval did not include zero, the effect size was significant.

Results

The first hypothesis held that acclaims would be more common than attacks in candidate election discourse. Sixteen message forms with a combined *n* of 184,995 were used for this analysis. The weighted mean effect size corrected for measurement error (*r*) was .5, which was significant. See Table 2 for these data.

Hypothesis 2 expected that candidates for elective office would discuss policy more often than character. This analysis employed data from 15 message forms with a combined *n* of 179,228. The weighted mean corrected effect size was .42, which was significant. These data are displayed in Table 3.

The third prediction anticipated that incumbents would acclaim more, and attack less, than challengers. The weighted effect size corrected for measurement error was .14, which was not was statistically significant. These data are reported in Table 4.

The next hypothesis (H4) also contrasted messages from incumbents and challengers but limited its scope to comments about the two candidates' records in office (past deeds). It is based on nine message forms with a combined *n* of 20,937. The relationship between function and incumbency here was significant: The corrected weighted mean *r* was .59. These data can be found in Table 5.

The fifth hypothesis contrasts the function of utterances from incumbents versus challengers that address future plans (specific policy proposals). When talking about their future plans, challengers are more likely to acclaim, and less likely to attack, than incumbents. Data from eight message forms with a combined *n* of 7,692 contributed to this analysis. Each message form found a significant effect but the weighted effect size corrected for measurement error here is .09, which was not significant. See Table 6.

Table 3. Topics of Political Campaign Messages.

Message	Policy	Character	χ^2	*n*	Corrected *r*
Announcement Speeches	3833 (54%)	3303 (46%)	39.22	7136	.08
Acceptance Addresses	1887 (54%)	1586 (46%)	25.92	3473	.15
Primary Brochures	6020 (62%)	3626 (38%)	594.16	9646	.3
General Brochures	8848 (77%)	2699 (23%)	3273.4	11547	.6
Primary Spots	4253 (54%)	3563 (46%)	60.74	7816	.1
General Spots	4540 (61%)	2894 (39%)	364.45	7434	.23
Primary Debates	25226 (69%)	11166 (31%)	5431.38	36392	.48
General Debates	6567 (74%)	2284 (26%)	2072.58	8851	.59
Primary Webpages	9658 (73%)	3485 (37%)	2898.4	13143	.54
General Webpages	10779 (81%)	2474 (19%)	5204.33	13253	.73
Vice Presidential Debates	3455 (68%)	1597 (32%)	682.6	5052	.41
Non-Presidential Spots	12071 (56%)	9644 (44%)	271.04	21715	.12
Non-Presidential Debates	6835 (72%)	2693 (28%)	1799.74	9528	.48
Mayoral Webpages	4277 (71%)	1769 (29%)	1039.54	6046	.45
Non-U.S. Debates	13515 (74%)	4681 (26%)	4287.86	18196	.54
Total *n*	weighted corrected *r*	*sd*			
179,228	.42	.21	$p < .05$		

Hypotheses six and seven contrasted the content of primary versus general campaign messages. H6 addressed the functions of these two groups of messages. Six message forms with a combined *n* of 122,567 provided data for this analysis. The corrected weighted mean effect size is .1, which is significant. See Table 7 for these data.

Hypothesis seven concerned the topics of primary versus general campaign message. The analysis was based on data from six message forms with an *n* of 124,308. The weighted mean effect size corrected for measurement error was .16, a significant relationship. These data are reported in Table 8.

H8 limited its analysis to candidates' utterances on general goals. Data were obtained from 15 studies which had a sample size of 53,015. The corrected weighted mean *r* was .89 and this result was statistically significant. See Table 9 for these data.

The next prediction (H9) limited its analysis to statements about ideals. Fifteen message forms with a combined *n* of 13,439 produced a weighted corrected mean effect size of .77. This was significant. These data are displayed in Table 10.

Table 4. Functions of Incumbents versus Challengers in Political Campaign Messages.

	Acclaims	Attacks	χ^2	*n*	Corrected *r*
Acceptance Addresses					
Incumbents	**1534 (83%)**	317 (17%)	93.15	3473	.18
Challengers	1118 (68%)	**504 (31%)**			
Brochures					
Incumbents	**4152 (77%)**	1218 (23%)	222.82	11547	.15
Challengers	3997 (65%)	**2180 (35%)**			
US Presidential Spots					
Incumbents	**2078 (59%)**	1471 (41%)	39.36	7025	.07
Challengers	1773 (51%)	**1700 (49%)**			
US Presidential Debates					
Incumbents	**2458 (70%)**	1031 (30%)	197.79	7758	.18
Challengers	2342 (55%)	**1927 (45%)**			
US Vice Presidential Debates					
Incumbents	**1568 (63%)**	915 (37%)	24.31	4965	.07
Challengers	1397 (56%)	**1085 (44%)**			
Non-Presidential Spots					
Incumbents	**6464 (83%)**	1289 (17%)	1472.72	18078	.31
Challengers	5831 (57%)	**4404 (43%)**			
US Non-Presidential Debates					
Incumbents	**1982 (75%)**	662 (25%)	137.15	5594	.17
Challengers	1777 (60%)	**1173 (40%)**			
Mayoral Webpages					
Incumbents	819 (100%)	2 (0.4%)	419.81	1777	.96
Challengers	700 (73%)	256 (27%)			
Non-US Debates					
Incumbents	**2634 (67%)**	1288 (33%)	158.93	9943	.14
Challengers	3279 (52%)	**2742 (43%)**			
Total *n*	weighted corrected *r*	*sd*			
70,160	.14	.3	*ns*		

Table 5. Functions of Incumbents versus Challengers on Past Deeds in Political Campaign Messages.

	Acclaims	Attacks	χ^2	*n*	Corrected *r*
Acceptance Addresses					
Incumbents	**321 (74%)**	110 (26%)	241.98	749	.62
Challengers	54 (17%)	**264 (83%)**			
Brochures					
Incumbents	**1994 (76%)**	613 (24%)	927.38	4615	.59
Challengers	637 (32%)	**1371 (68%)**			
Spots					
Incumbents	**542 (49%)**	568 (51%)	192.66	2257	.32
Challengers	241 (21%)	**906 (79%)**			
Debates					
Incumbents	**799 (69%)**	362 (31%)	695.43	2556	.6
Challengers	242 (17%)	**1153 (83%)**			
Vice Presidential Debates					
Incumbents	**514 (62%)**	318 (38%)	354.38	1831	.48
Challengers	188 (19%)	**811 (81%)**			
Non-Presidential Spots					
Incumbents	**1582 (75%)**	539 (25%)	703.55	3778	.48
Challengers	520 (31%)	**1137 (69%)**			
Non-Presidential Debates					
Incumbents	**716 (76%)**	229 (24%)	452.12	1836	.55
Challengers	233 (26%)	**658 (74%)**			
Mayoral Webpages					
Incumbents	445 (100%)	2 (0.4%)	419.81	586	.88
Challengers	30 (22%)	109 (78%)			
Non-US Debates					
Incumbents	**656 (63%)**	383 (37%)	474.16	2729	.47
Challengers	365 (22%)	**1325 (78%)**			
Total *n*	weighted corrected *r*	*sd*			
20,937	.59	.15	$p < .05$		

Table 6. Functions of Incumbents versus Challengers on Future Plans in Political Campaign Messages.

	Acclaims	Attacks	χ^2	*n*	Corrected *r*
Acceptance Addresses					
Incumbents	108 (73%)	**40 (27%)**	8.59	226	.22
Challengers	**70 (90%)**	8 (10%)			
Brochures					
Incumbents	613 (71%)	**249 (29%)**	8.53	1344	.1
Challengers	**378 (78%)**	104 (22%)			
US Presidential Spots					
Incumbents	180 (42%)	**253 (58%)**	10.91	911	.12
Challengers	**251 (53%)**	227 (47%)			
US Presidential Debates					
Incumbents	377 (61%)	**239 (39%)**	19.78	1293	.14
Challengers	**493 (73%)**	184 (27%)			
US Vice Presidential Debates					
Incumbents	70 (39%)	**109 (61%)**	7.29	335	.16
Challengers	**84 (54%)**	72 (46%)			
Non-Presidential Spots					
Incumbents	187 (68%)	**89 (32%)**	151.29	1096	.42
Challengers	**781 (81%)**	39 (19%)			
Non-Presidential Debates					
Incumbents	24 (55%)	**20 (45%)**	4.27	94	.23
Challengers	**68 (72%)**	26 (28%)			
Mayoral Webpages					
Incumbents	37 (100%)	0	†		
Challengers	135 (95%)	7 (5%)			
Non-US Debates					
Incumbents	646 (68%)	**298 (32%)**	15.6	2393	.09
Challengers	**1098 (76%)**	351 (24%)			
Total *n*	weighted *r*	*sd*			
7,692	.09	.11	*ns*		

†Data does not meet assumptions necessary to calculate χ^2.

Table 7. Functions of Primary versus General Political Campaign Messages.

	Acclaims	Attacks	χ^2	*n*	Corrected *r*
Brochures					
Primary	**8207 (84%)**	1526 (16%)	561.35	21280	.17
General	8149 (71%)	**3398 (29%)**			
Presidential Spots					
Primary	**5630 (72%)**	2186 (28%)	516.12	15160	.2
General	3983 (54%)	**3361 (46%)**			
Presidential Debates					
Primary	**21901 (66%)**	9666 (29%)	161.05	39325	.07
General	4800 (57%)	**2958 (35%)**			
Webpages					
Primary	**14308 (94%)**	972 (6%)	56.35	28544	.04
General	12110 (91%)	**1154 (9%)**			
Non-Presidential Spots					
Primary	**3024 (73%)**	1115 (27%)	27.28	8476	.06
General	2944 (69%)	**1393 (31%)**			
Non-Presidential Debates					
Primary	**699 (71%)**	211 (22%)	98.63	9871	.11
General	5377 (58%)	**3584 (37%)**			
Total *n*	weighted corrected *r*	*sd*			
122,567	.1	.06	$p < .05$		

The eighth prediction contrasted the functions of candidate utterances on future plans (specific plans, means) versus general goals (ends). Fifteen messages forms contributed data representing an *n* of 72,770. The corrected weighted mean effect size obtained was .16, which did not reach significance. Table 11 displays these data.

The final hypothesis anticipated that campaign messages from candidates have more acclaims and fewer attacks than those from other sources (e.g., surrogates, outside groups). Eight unique datasets with a combined *n* of 19,851 yielded a weighted corrected effect size of .18, which was significant. See Table 12 for these data.

Discussion and Conclusion

The Functional Theory of Political Campaign Discourse was developed to help understand certain elements (functions, topics) of candidate election messages. It

Table 8. Topics of Primary versus General Political Campaign Messages.

	Policy	Character	χ^2	*n*	Corrected *r*
Brochures					
Primary	6020 (62%)	**3626 (38%)**	507.33	21193	.16
General	**8848 (77%)**	2699 (23%)			
Presidential Spots					
Primary	4253 (54%)	**3563 (46%)**	69.16	15259	.08
General	**4540 (61%)**	2894 (39%)			
Presidential Debates					
Primary	25226 (69%)	**11166 (31%)**	81.08	45243	.04
General	**6567 (74%)**	2284 (26%)			
Webpages					
Primary	9658 (73%)	**3485 (27%)**	233.31	26394	.1
General	**10779 (81%)**	2472 (19%)			
Non-Presidential Spots					
Primary	1840 (48%)	**1979 (52%)**	73.09	7422	.11
General	**2093 (58%)**	1510 (42%)			
Non-Presidential Debates					
Primary	531 (60%)	**349 (40%)**	52.45	8797	.09
General	**5703 (72%)**	2214 (28%)			
Total *n*	weighted corrected *r*	*sd*			
124,308	.16	.04	$p < .05$		

has been employed to analyze campaign messages representing many candidates, many years, multiple offices, in the U.S. and other countries.

This meta-analysis investigated ten of Functional Theory's predictions, eight of which were confirmed. Acclaims are more common than attacks. Attacks are risky because many voters report that they do not like mudslinging; a backlash against a candidate can ensue after that candidate attacks an opponent. Candidates for elective office discuss policy more than character. Some voters view political leaders (such as presidents, prime ministers, chancellors, senators, governors, mayors) as personal role models; however, it seems that more voters see these leaders as policy makers. Perhaps responding to voter preferences, most candidates discuss policy more than character. Candidates' record in office (past deeds) is an important variable in campaigns: Both incumbents and challengers discussed the incumbent's record more than they talked about the challenger's record. Of course, incumbents acclaim when talking about their record whereas challengers attack

Table 9. Functions of General Goals in Political Campaign Messages.

Message	Acclaims	Attacks	χ^2	*n*	Corrected *r*
Announcement Speeches	**1829 (92%)**	153 (8%)	1417.24	1982	.92
Acceptance Addresses	**649 (92%)**	56 (8%)	498.79	705	.91
Primary Brochures	**2886 (95%)**	147 (5%)	2473.5	3033	.99
General Brochures	**2903 (88%)**	399 (12%)	1898.85	3302	.9
Primary TV Spots	**1776 (90%)**	199 (10%)	1259.2	1975	.91
General TV Spots	**1129 (82%)**	243 (18%)	572.15	1372	.71
Primary Debates	**14867 (91%)**	1468 (9%)	10981.03	16325	.96
General Debates	**2041 (85%)**	360 (15%)	1176.91	2401	.8
Primary Webpages	**4902 (98%)**	103 (2%)	4599.56	5005	.99
General Webpages	**3559 (96%)**	1154 (4%)	1226.22	4713	.57
Vice Presidential Debates	**1042 (81%)**	247 (19%)	490.32	1289	.68
Non-Presidential Spots	**1922 (88%)**	264 (12%)	1257.53	2186	.85
Non-Presidential Debates	**3172 (88%)**	427 (12%)	2093.64	3599	.84
Mayoral Webpages	**1914 (98%)**	36 (2%)	1808.66	1950	.99
Non-U.S. Debates	**2674 (84%)**	504 (16%)	1481.72	3178	.81
Total *n*	weighted corrected *r*	*sd*			
53,015	.89	.14	$p < .05$		

when discussing the incumbent's record. Messages from candidates feature fewer attacks than those from others.

Election messages employed in the primary phase of a campaign differ from those crafted for the general campaign. Primary messages acclaim more and attack less than general messages; general campaign messages discuss policy more, and character less, than primary elections. For example, in general, more policy differences (opportunities to attack) occur more between candidates of different political parties (general campaigns) than between candidates from the same party. Furthermore, candidates are less well-known in the primary than the general campaign, encouraging more character discussion in the primary than the general campaign. Both general goals (e.g., creating more jobs) and ideals (freedom) are easier to acclaim than to attack. It is important to note that bias could influence interpretation of these results.

Three predictions were not confirmed: that incumbents emphasize different functions than challengers (H3), that challengers acclaim more and attack less than incumbents when discussing future plans (H5) and that candidates will acclaim more and attack less on future plans than general goals (H10). Two variables are used to determine whether the relationship is significant (to determine

Table 10. Functions of Ideals in Political Campaign Messages.

Message	Acclaims	Attacks	χ^2	*n*	Corrected *r*
Announcement Speeches	**1415 (91%)**	134 (9%)	1059.37	1549	.95
Acceptance Addresses	**646 (85%)**	114 (15%)	512.82	695	.99
Primary Brochures	**528 (92%)**	49 (8%)	397.64	577	.99
General Brochures	**446 (81%)**	106 (19%)	209.42	552	.7
Primary TV Spots	**652 (89%)**	81 (11%)	444.8	733	.84
General TV Spots	**386 (78%)**	108 (22%)	156.45	494	.63
Primary Debates	**3370 (88%)**	443 (12%)	1230.35	2713	.78
General Debates	**534 (82%)**	120 (18%)	262.07	654	.67
Primary Webpages	**1819 (95%)**	86 (5%)	1574.72	1905	.99
General Webpages	**922 (97%)**	32 (3%)	828.42	954	.94
Vice Presidential Debates	**169 (78%)**	49 (22%)	66.06	218	.62
Non-Presidential Spots	**573 (83%)**	114 (17%)	306.67	687	.74
Non-Presidential Debates	**351 (85%)**	62 (15%)	202.23	413	.81
Mayoral Webpages	**630 (97%)**	19 (3%)	575.22	649	.96
Non-U.S. Debates	**544 (84%)**	102 (16%)	302.42	646	.77
Total *n*	weighted corrected *r*	*sd*			
13,439	.77	.14	$p < .05$		

the size of the confidence interval): (corrected) weighted mean effect size and the standard deviation, so failure to reach significance could be attributed to one of these three variables. The effect sizes for H3 ranged from 0.07 to .96; for H5 it varied from −0.09 to .42; for H10 it ran from −0.01 to .38. It seems likely that the failure to reach significance in all three cases are due at least in part to the high *standard deviation* for these variables. As noted above, Functional Theory does not make assertions about what candidates *must* say in their messages: Candidates and their advisors decide what to discuss in their messages; these hypotheses embody reasons rather than causes. It is also possible that bias influenced interpretation of the data.

A further possible explanation for the failure to confirm prediction H3 can be found in cross pressures acting on these candidates. H4 (incumbency and past deeds) and H5 (incumbency and future plans) show that incumbents and challengers are subject to cross pressures. Compared with challengers, incumbents *acclaim more* (71% to 23%) and *attack less* (29% to 73%) on past deeds; incumbents *attack more* (42% to 23%) and *acclaim less* (58% to 77%) on future plans. The former relationship is stronger than the latter but these factors incline candidates in opposite ways when it comes to the functions of their campaign messages.

Table 11. Functions of Future Plans versus General Goals in Political Campaign Messages.

	Acclaims	Attacks	χ^2	n	Corrected r
Announcement Speeches					
Future Plans	392 (89%)	**48 (11%)**	4.81	2422	.04
General Goals	**1829 (92%)**	153 (8%)			
Acceptance Addresses					
Future Plans	178 (79%)	**48 (21%)**	30.49	931	.2
General Goals	**649 (92%)**	56 (8%)			
Primary Brochures					
Future Plans	505 (89%)	**64 (11%)**	35.6	3602	.11
General Goals	**2886 (95%)**	147 (5%)			
General Brochures					
Future Plans	755 (81%)	**176 (19%)**	28.78	4233	.1
General Goals	**2903 (88%)**	399 (12%)			
Presidential Primary Spots					
Future Plans	404 (72%)	**154 (28%)**	111.38	2533	.24
General Goals	**1776 (90%)**	199 (10%)			
Presidential Spots					
Future Plans	431 (47%)	**480 (53%)**	309.53	2283	.4
General Goals	**1129 (82%)**	243 (18%)			
Presidential Primary Debates					
Future Plans	2581 (72%)	**1016 (28%)**	1002.25	19932	.26
General Goals	**14867 (91%)**	1468 (9%)			
US Presidential Debates					
Future Plans	870 (67%)	**423 (33%)**	158	3694	.24
General Goals	**2041 (85%)**	360 (15%)			
US Vice Presidential Debates					
Future Plans	154 (46%)	**181 (54%)**	166.55	1624	.38
General Goals	**1042 (81%)**	247 (19%)			
Primary Webpages					
Future Plans	3049 (95%)	**144 (5%)**	40.11	8198	.08
General Goals	**4902 (98%)**	103 (2%)			
General Webpages					
Future Plans	2334 (96%)	94 (4%)	.34	6142	-.01
General Goals	3559 (96%)	155 (4%)			

(continued)

Table 11. *continued*

	Acclaims	Attacks	χ^2	*n*	Corrected *r*
VP Debates					
Future Plans	154 (46%)	**181 (54%)**	166.55	1624	.35
General Goals	**1042 (81%)**	247 (19%)			
Non-Presidential Debates					
Future Plans	444 (74%)	**158 (26%)**	88.99	4201	.16
General Goals	**3172 (88%)**	427 (12%)			
Non-Presidential Spots					
Future Plans	642 (72%)	**245 (28%)**	134.99	3684	.21
General Goals	**2476 (89%)**	321 (11%)			
Mayoral Webpages					
Future Plans	1094 (99%)	9 (1%)	5.15	3053	-0.04
General Goals	1914 (98%)	36 (2%)			
Non-US Debates					
Future Plans	1037 (72%)	**399 (28%)**	89.38	4614	.16
General Goals	**2674 (84%)**	504 (16%)			
Total *n*	weighted corrected *r*	*Sd*			
72,770	.16	.12	*ns*		

Political communication scholars should continue to investigate other theories: Functional Theory does not pretend to answer every question about election messages: For example, it does not analyze metaphors or visual elements of election messages. It does discuss such ideas as functions and topics, incumbency, and campaign phase. This theory has strong predictive value for some elements of election campaign messages; further research here would be useful. Campaign messages using other message forms (e.g., candidate Facebook pages or tweets), other elective offices (e.g., U.S. House of Representatives debates), and other countries could prove useful. Some research has investigated television spots from other countries (see, e.g., Benoit, 2014a) but only political leaders' debates outside the U.S. have received sustained attention from Functional Theory. Further research can also provide additional data on trends over time because the content of election messages could shift over time. For example, Benoit and Compton (2016) report that presidential TV spots had a sharp uptick in attacks

Table 12. Functions and Source of Campaign Message.

	Acclaims	Attacks	χ^2	*n*	Corrected *r*
2000 Presidential					
Candidate	221 (73%)	79 (26%)	63.3	4195	φ = .35
Party	107 (40%)	157 (59%)			
2000 Senate					
Candidate	927 (78%)	255 (22%)	196.12	1414	φ = .38
Party	76 (32%)	156 (67%)	κ = .96		
2000 House					
Candidate	318 (70%)	135 (30%)	46.65	530	φ = .31
Party	23 (30%)	54 (70%)			
2004 President					
Candidate	370 (52%)	343 (48%)	123.81	1219	φ = .34
PACs	104 (20%)	405 (80%)			
2004 Non-President					
Candidate	4076 (74%)	1648 (26%	152.04	6080	φ =.17
Party + PAC	143 (40%)	213 (60%)			
2008 Senate + Governor					
Candidate	883 (66%)	450 (34%)	19.49	1456	φ = .13
Party	57 (46%)	66 (54%)			
2016 Presidential Primary					
Candidate	1016 (77%)	295 (23%)	28.79	2181	φ = .12
PAC	584 (67%)	286 (33%)			
1960–1996 Convention Speeches					
Acceptances	1359 (74%)	480 (26%)	150.39	2776	φ =.23
Keynotes	474 (51%)	463 (49%)			
Total *n*	weighted corrected *r*	*sd*			
19,851	.18	.1	$p < .05$		

in 2008 and 2012, compared with earlier campaigns. Only longitudinal research can determine whether shifts in functions or topics have occurred over time. Research into the audience effects of functions and topics (e.g., Reinemann & Maurer, 2005) would be very helpful. This theory deserves further attention from scholars.

References

*Airne, D., & Benoit, W. L. (2005). Political television advertising in campaign 2000. *Communication Quarterly, 53*, 473–492.

Atkin, C. K. (1977). Effects of campaign advertising and newscasts on children. *Journalism Quarterly, 54*, 503–508.

Atkin, C. K., & Heald, G. (1976). Effects of political advertising. *Public Opinion Quarterly, 40*, 216–228.

Baker, K. L., & Norpoth, H. (1981). Candidates on television: The 1972 electoral debates in West Germany. Public Opinion Quarterly, *45*, 329–345.

Basil, M., Schooler, C., & Reeves, B. (1991). Positive and negative political advertising: Effectiveness of ads and perceptions of candidates. In F. Biocca (Ed.), *Television and political advertising* (vol. 1, pp. 245–262). Hillsdale, NJ: Erlbaum.

Becker, L. B., & Doolittle, J. C. (1975). How repetition affects evaluations of and information seeking about candidates. *Journalism Quarterly, 52*, 611–617.

Benoit, W. L. (2003). Topic of presidential campaign discourse and election outcome. *Western Journal of Communication, 67*, 97–112.

Benoit, W. L. (2007). *Communication in political campaigns*. New York: Peter Lang.

*Benoit, W. L. (2011). A Functional analysis of the English language 2011 Canadian Prime Minister debate. *Contemporary Argumentation and Debate, 32*, 45–69.

Benoit, W. L. (2013). Mudslinging: The nature of attacks in political campaigns. In C. Rountree (Ed.), *Venomous speech and other problems in American political discourse* (pp. 129–147). Westport, CT: Praeger.

*Benoit, W. L. (2014a). *A functional analysis of presidential television advertisements* (2nd ed.). Lanham, MD: Lexington Books.

*Benoit, W. L. (2014b). A Functional analysis of 2008 and 2012 presidential nomination acceptance addresses. *Speaker & Gavel, 51*, 50–59.

*Benoit, W. L. (2014c). *Political election debates: Informing voters about policy and character*. Lanham, MD: Lexington Books.

*Benoit, W. L., & Airne, D. (2009). A functional analysis of non-presidential TV spots in campaign 2004. *Human Communication, 12*, 91–117.

*Benoit, W. L., & Airne, D. (2013). A functional analysis of non-presidential TV spots in campaign 2002. *Unpublished paper.*

Benoit, W. L., & Benoit-Bryan, J. M. (2013). Debates come to the UK: A Functional analysis of the 2010 British Prime Minister election debates. *Communication Quarterly, 61*, 463–478.

*Benoit, W. L., & Benoit-Bryan, J. M. (2014a). A Functional analysis of the 2010 Australian Prime Minister debate. *Journal of Argumentation in Context, 3*, 153–168.

*Benoit, W. L., & Benoit-Bryan, J. M. (2014b). A Functional analysis of UK debates in Northern Ireland, Scotland, and Wales. *Western Journal of Communication, 78*, 653–667.

*Benoit, W. L., & Benoit-Bryan, J. M. (2015). A Functional analysis of 2013 Australian member of parliament and prime minister debates. *Studies in Media and Communication, 3*, 1–8.

*Benoit, W. L., Brazeal, L. M., & Airne, D. (2007). A Functional analysis of televised U.S. Senate and gubernatorial campaign debates. *Argumentation and Advocacy, 44*, 75–89.

*Benoit, W. L., & Compton, J. (2016). Functions and topics of 2012 American presidential advertising: An increase in attacks? *Journal of Mass Communication and Journalism, 6*, 297–303.

Benoit, W. L., Compton, J., & Phillips, B. (2013). Newspaper coverage of Prime Minister elections in Australia, Canada, and the United Kingdom. *Human Communication, 16*, 201–213.

*Benoit, W. L., Delbert, J., Sudbrock, L. A., & Vogt, C. (2010). Functional analysis of 2008 senate and gubernatorial TV spots. *Human Communication, 13*, 103–125.

Benoit, W. L., Furgerson, J., Seifert, J., & Sargardia, S. (2013). Newspaper coverage of senate, gubernatorial, and mayoral elections. *Human Communication, 16*, 215–229.

*Benoit, W. L., & Glantz, M. (2015). A Functional analysis of 2012 United States general election presidential and vice presidential debates. In C. Bieber & K. Kamps (Eds.), *Die US-präsidentschaftswahl 2012* (pp. 289–306). Wiesboden: Springer.

*Benoit, W. L., Glantz, M., & Rill, L. (2016). Campaigning on the Internet: 2008 presidential general election candidate webpages. *Unpublished paper.*

Benoit, W. L., Hansen, G. J., & Holbert, R. L. (2004). Presidential campaigns and democracy. *Mass Communication and Society, 7*, 177–190.

Benoit, W. L., Hansen, G. J., & Verser, R. M. (2003). A meta-analysis of the effects of viewing U.S. presidential debates. *Communication Monographs, 70*, 335–350.

*Benoit, W. L., & Hemmer, K. (2007). *A functional analysis of German chancellor debates, 2002 and 2005.* San Francisco, CA: ICA.

Benoit, W. L., Hemmer, K., & Stein, K. (2010). *New York Times'* coverage of American presidential primary campaigns, 1952-2004. *Human Communication, 13*, 259–280.

*Benoit, W. L., & Henson, J. R. (2007). A Functional analysis of the 2006 Canadian and 2007 Australian election debates. *Argumentation & Advocacy, 44*, 36–48.

*Benoit, W. L., Henson, J., Davis, C., Glantz, M., Phillips, A., & Rill, L. (2013). Stumping on the Internet: 2008 presidential primary candidate campaign webpages. *Human Communication, 16*, 1–12.

*Benoit, W. L., Henson, J. R., & Maltos, S. (2007). A Functional analysis of mayoral debates. *Contemporary Argumentation and Debate, 28*, 20–37.

*Benoit, W. L., Henson, J., Whalen, S., & Pier, P. M. (2008). "I am a candidate for president": A functional analysis of presidential announcement speeches, 1960-2004. *Speaker & Gavel, 45*, 3–18.

*Benoit, W. L., & Klyukovski, A. A. (2006). A Functional analysis of 2004 Ukrainian presidential debates. *Argumentation, 20*, 209–225.

Benoit, W. L., Leshner, G. M., & Chattopadhyay, S. (2007). A meta-analysis of political advertising. *Human Communication, 10*, 507–522.

*Benoit, W. L., McHale, J. P., Hansen, G. J., Pier, P. M., & McGuire, J. P. (2003). *Campaign 2000: A functional analysis of presidential campaign discourse.* Lanham, MD: Rowman & Littlefield.

Benoit, W. L., McKinney, M. S., & Holbert, R. L. (2001). Beyond learning and persona: Extending the scope of presidential debate effects. *Communication Monographs, 68,* 259–273.

Benoit, W. L., McKinney, M. S., & Stephenson, M. T. (2002). Effects of watching campaign 2000 presidential primary debates. *Journal of Communication, 52,* 316–331.

*Benoit, W. L., & Sheafer, T. (2006). Functional theory and political discourse: Televised debates in Israel and the United States. *Journalism & Mass Communication Quarterly, 83,* 281–297.

*Benoit, W. L., & Stein, K. A. (2005). A Functional analysis of presidential direct mail advertising. *Communication Studies, 56,* 203–225.

Benoit, W. L., Stein, K. A., & Hansen, G. J. (2005). *New York Times* coverage of presidential campaigns, 1952-2000. *Journalism & Mass Communication Quarterly, 82,* 356–376.

*Benoit, W. L., Stein, K. A., McHale, J. P., Chattopadhyay, S., Verser, R., & Price, S. (2007). *Bush versus Kerry: A functional analysis of campaign 2004.* New York: Peter Lang.

Benoit, W. L., & Stephenson, M. T. (2004). Effects of watching a presidential primary debate. *Contemporary Argumentation and Debate, 25,* 1–25.

Benoit, W. L., Webber, D., & Berman, J. (1998). Effects of presidential debate watching and ideology on attitudes and knowledge. *Argumentation and Advocacy, 34,* 163–172.

*Benoit, W. L., & Wells, W. T. (1996). *Candidates in conflict: Persuasive attack and defense in the 1992 presidential debates.* Tuscaloosa: University of Alabama Press.

*Benoit, W. L., Wells, W. T., Pier, P. M., & Blaney, J. R. (1999). Acclaiming, attacking, and defending in presidential nomination convention acceptance addresses, 1960-1996. *Quarterly Journal of Speech, 85,* 247–267.

Blumler, J. G. (2011). Voters' responses to the Prime Minister debates: A rock of (future?) ages. In S. Coleman (Ed.), *Leaders in the living room: The prime ministerial debates of 2010: Evidence, evaluation, and some recommendations* (pp. 35–54). Oxford: Reuters Institute for the Study of Journalism.

Brazeal, L. M., & Benoit, W. L. (2001). A Functional analysis of Congressional television spots, 1986-2000. *Communication Quarterly, 49,* 436–454. DOI: 10.1080/01463370109385640.

*Brazeal, L. M., & Benoit, W. L. (2006). On the spot: A Functional analysis of congressional television spots, 1980-2004. *Communication Studies, 57,* 401–420.

Broder, D. (2002, October 6). Congress can't recognize vital issues. *Spokesman-Review.* Accessed 5/17/16: https://news.google.com/newspapers?nid=1314&dat=20021006&id=5LszAAAAIBAJ&sjid=rPIDAAAAIBAJ&pg=2818,4320236&hl=en

*Choi, Y. S., & Benoit, W. L. (2009). A Functional analysis of French and South Korean debates. *Speaker & Gavel, 46,* 59–78.

*Choi, Y. S., & Benoit, W. L. (2013). A Functional analysis of the 2007 and 2012 French presidential debates. *Journal of Intercultural Communication Research, 42,* 215–227.

Clarke, P., & Evans, S. H. (1983). *Covering campaigns: Journalism in congressional elections.* Stanford, CA: Stanford University Press.

Cohen, J. (1960). A coefficient of agreement for nominal scales. *Educational and Psychological Measurement, 20*, 37–46.

Christ, W. B., Thorson, E., & Caywood, C. (1994). Do attitudes toward political advertising affect information processing of televised political commercials? *Journal of Broadcasting & Electronic Media, 38*, 251–270.

Cundy, D. T. (1986). Political commercials and candidate image: The effect can be substantial. In L. L. Kaid, D. Nimmo, & K. R. Sanders (Eds.), *New perspectives on political advertising* (pp. 210–234). Carbondale: Southern Illinois Press.

Damore, D. E. (2002). Candidate strategy and the decision to go negative. *Political Research Quarterly, 55*, 669–685.

Davis, J. W. (1997). *U.S. presidential primaries and the caucus-convention system*. Westport, CT: Greenwood Press.

Donohue, T. R. (1973). Viewer perceptions of color and black-and-white paid political advertising. *Journalism Quarterly, 50*, 660–665.

Dover, E. D. (2006). *Images, issues, and attacks: Television advertising by incumbents and challengers in presidential elections*. Lanham, MD: Rowman & Littlefield.

Dudek, P., & Partacz, S. (2009). Functional theory of political discourse: Televised debates during the parliamentary campaign in 2007 in Poland. *Central European Journal of Communication, 2*, 367–379.

Elmelund-Praestekaer, C. (2010). Beyond American negativity: Toward a general understanding of the determinants of negative campaigning. *European Political Science Review, 2*, 137–156.

Faber, R. J., & Storey, M. C. (1984). Recall of information from political advertising. *Journal of Advertising, 13*, 39–44.

Faber, R. J., Tims, A. R., & Schmitt, K. G. (1993). Negative political advertising and voting intent: The role of involvement and alternative information sources. *Journal of Advertising, 22*, 67–76.

Franz, M. M., Freedman, P. B., Goldstein, K. M., & Ridout, T. N. (2008). *Campaign advertising and American democracy*. Philadelphia, PA: Temple University Press.

Garramone, G. M. (1984). Voter responses to negative political ads. *Journalism Quarterly, 61*, 250–269.

Garramone, G. M. (1985). Effects of negative political advertising: The roles of sponsor and rebuttal. *Journal of Broadcasting and Electronic Media, 29*, 147–159.

Garramone, G. M., Atkin, C. K., Pinkleton, B. E., & Cole, R. T. (1990). Effects of negative political advertising on the political process. *Journal of Broadcasting and Electronic Media, 34*, 299–311.

Garramone, G. M., & Smith, S. J. (1984). Reactions to political advertising: Clarifying sponsor effects. *Journalism Quarterly, 51*, 771–775.

Geiger, S. F., & Reeves, B. (1991). The effects of visual structure and content emphasis on the evaluation and memory for political candidates. In F. Biocca (Ed.), *Television and political advertising* (vol. 1, pp. 125–143). Hillsdale, NJ: Erlbaum.

Geer, J. G. (2006). *In defense of negativity: Attack ads in presidential campaigns*. Chicago, IL: University of Chicago Press.

*Glantz, M., Delbert, J., & Davis, C. (2016). A Functional Analysis of 2013 mayoral campaign web pages. *Speaker & Gavel, 53*, 43–63.

Glass, G. V., McGaw, B., & Smith, M. L. (1981). *Meta-analysis in social research*. Beverly Hills, CA: Sage Publications.

Gordon, B. R., & Hartmann, W. R. (2013). Advertising effects in presidential elections. *Marketing Science, 32*, 19–35.

Hill, R. P. (1989). An exploration of voter responses to political advertisements. *Journal of Advertising, 18*, 14–22.

Hitchon, J. C., & Chang, C. (1995). Effects of gender schematic processing on the reception of political commercials for men and women candidates. *Communication Research, 22*, 430–458.

Hofstetter, C. R. (1976). *Bias in the news: Network television coverage of the 1972 election campaign*. Columbus, OH: Ohio State University Press.

Hunter, J. E., & Schmidt, F. L. (1990). *Methods of meta-analysis: Correcting error and bias in research findings*. Newbury Park, CA: Sage Publications.

Hunter, J. E., & Schmidt, F. L. (2004). *Methods of meta-analysis: Correcting error and bias in research findings* (2nd ed.). Thousand Oaks, CA: Sage.

Jarman, J. W. (2005). Political affiliation and presidential debates: A real-time analysis of the effect of arguments used in the presidential debates. *American Behavioral Scientist, 49*, 229–242.

Johnston, D. D. (1989). Image and issue political information: Message content or interpretation? *Journalism Quarterly, 66*, 379–382.

Joslyn, R. A. (1981). The impact of campaign spot advertising on voting defections. *Human Communication Research, 7*, 347–360.

Just, M., Crigler, A., & Wallach, L. (1990). Thirty seconds or thirty minutes: What viewers learn from spot advertisements and candidate debates. *Journal of Communication, 40*, 120–132.

Kaid, L. L. (1994). Political advertising in the 1992 campaign. In R. E. Denton (Ed.), *The 1992 presidential campaign: A communication perspective* (pp. 111–127). Westport, CT: Praeger.

Kaid, L. L. (1997). Effects of the television spots on images of Dole and Clinton. *American Behavioral Scientist, 40*, 1085–1094.

Kaid, L. L., & Boydston, J. (1987). An experimental study of the effectiveness of negative political advertisements. *Communication Quarterly, 35*, 193–201.

Kaid, L. L., & Holtz-Bacha, C. (Eds.). (2006). *The Sage handbook of political advertising*. Thousand Oaks, CA: Sage.

Kaid, L. L., & Johnston, A. (1991). Negative versus positive television advertising in U.S. presidential campaigns, 1960-1988. *Journal of Communication, 41*, 53–64.

Kaid, L. L., & Johnston, A. (2001). *Videostyle in presidential campaigns Style and content of televised political advertising*. Westport, CT: Praeger.

Kaid, L. L., Leland, C. M., & Whitney, S. (1992). The impact of televised political ads: Evoking viewer responses in the 1988 presidential campaign. *Southern Communication Journal, 57*, 285–295.

Kaid, L. L., & Sanders, K. R. (1978). Political television commercials: An experimental study of type and length. *Communication Research, 5*, 57–70.

Kamber, V. (1997). *Poison politics: Are negative campaigns destroying democracy?* Cambridge, MA: Perseus.

King, A. (2002). Conclusions and implications. In A. King (Ed.), *Leaders' personalities and the outcomes of democratic elections* (pp. 210–221). Oxford: University Press.

Holbrook, T. M. (1996). *Do campaigns matter?* Thousand Oaks, CA: Sage.

Hrbkova, L., & Zagrapan, J. (2014). Slovak political debates: Functional theory in a multi-party system. *European Journal of Communication, 29*, 735–744.

Isotalus, P. (2011). Analyzing presidential debates: Functional theory and Finnish political communication culture. *Nordicom Review, 32*, 31–43.

Isotalus, P., & Aarnio, E. (2006). A model of televised election discussion: The Finnish multiparty system perspective. *Javnost-The Public, 13*, 61–72.

Kendall, K. E. (2000). *Communication in the presidential primaries: Candidates and the media, 1912-2000.* Westport, CT: Praeger.

Landis, J. R., & Koch, G. G. (1977). The measurement of observer agreement for categorical data. *Biometrica, 33*, 159–174.

Lang, A. (1991). Emotion, formal features, and memory for televised political advertisements. In F. Biocca (Ed.), *Television and political advertising* (vol. 1, pp. 221–243). Hillsdale, NJ: Erlbaum.

Lanoue, D. J. (1994). Retrospective and prospective voting in presidential year elections. *Political Research Quarterly, 47*, 193–205.

Lawless, J. L. (2012). *Becoming a candidate: Political ambition and the decision to run for office.* Cambridge: Cambridge University Press.

Loudan, A. (2016). Political communication. Accessed 6/15/16: http://users.wfu.edu/louden/Political%20Communication/poltitle.html

Maier, J., & Jansen, C. (2015). When do candidates attack in election campaigns? Exploring the determinants of negative candidate messages in German televised debates. *Party Politics, 21*, 1–11.

Mayer, W. G. (Ed.). (2000). *In pursuit of the White House: How we choose our presidential nominees* (pp. 203–253). New York: Chatham House.

McClure, R. D., & Patterson, T. E. (1974). Television news and political advertising: The impact of exposure on voter beliefs. *Communication Research, 1*, 3–21.

McKinney, M. S., & Carlin, D. B. (2004). Political campaign debates. In L. L. Kaid (Ed.), *Handbook of political campaign research* (pp. 203–234). Mahwah, NJ: Erlbaum.

Meadow, R. G., & Sigelman, L. (1982). Some effects and non-effects of campaign commercials: An experimental study. *Political Behavior, 4*, 163–175.

Merritt, S. (1984). Negative political advertising: Some empirical findings. *Journal of Advertising, 13*, 27–38.

Mulder, R. (1979). The effects of televised political ads in the 1975 Chicago mayoral election. *Journalism Quarterly, 56*, 335–341.

Nai, A., & Walter, A. S. (2015). The war of words: The art of negative campaigning. In A. Nai & A. S. Walter (Eds.), *New perspectives on negative campaigning: Why attack politics matter* (pp. 3–33). Colchester: ECPR.

Newhagen, J. E., & Reeves, B. (1991). Emotion and memory responses for negative political advertising: A study of television commercials used in the 1988 presidential election. In F. Biocca (Ed.), *Television and political advertising* (vol. 1, pp. 197–220). Hillsdale, NJ: Erlbaum.

Norrander, B. (2000). *The imperfect primary: Oddities, biases, and strengths of U.S. nomination politics.* New York: Routledge.

Palda, K. S. (1973). Does advertising influence votes? An analysis of the 1966 and 1970 Quebec elections. *Canadian Journal of Political Science, 6*, 638–655.

Palmer, N. A. (1997). *The New Hampshire primary and the American electoral process.* Westport, CT: Praeger.

Patterson, T. E. (2003). *The vanishing voter: Public involvement in an age of uncertainty.* New York: Random House, Vintage Books.

*Pier, P. M. (2002). *He said, she said: A functional analysis of gender differences in political campaign messages.* Unpublished doctoral dissertation, University of Missouri.

Racine Group. (2002). White paper on televised political campaign debates. *Argumentation and Advocacy, 38*, 199–218.

Reinemann, C., & Maurer, M. (2005). Unifying or polarizing? Short-term effects and post-debate consequences of different rhetorical strategies in televised debates. *Journal of Communication, 55*, 775–794.

Ridout, T. N., & Holland, J. L. (2010). Candidate strategies in the presidential nomination campaign. *Presidential Studies Quarterly, 40*, 611–630.

Roddy, B. L., & Garramone, G. M. (1988). Appeals and strategies of negative political advertising. *Journal of Broadcasting & Electronic Media, 32*, 415–427.

Rosenthal, R. (1991). *Meta-analytic procedures for social research* (rev. ed.). Newbury Park, CA: Sage.

Rudd, R. (1989). Effects of issue specificity, ambiguity on evaluations of candidate image. *Journalism Quarterly, 66*, 675–682, 691.

Salamore, S. A., & Salamore, B. G. (1995). *Campaigns, parties, and campaigns: Electoral politics in America.* Washington, DC: Congressional Quarterly Press.

Scammell, M., & Langer, A. I. (2006). Political advertising in the United Kingdom. In L. L. Kaid & C. Holtz-Bacha (Eds.). *The SAGE handbook of political advertising* (pp. 65–82). London: Sage.

Senior, P. (2008). Electoral impact of televised leaders' debates on Australian federal elections. *Australian Journal of Political Science, 43*, 443–464.

Shaw, D. R. (1999a). The effect of TV ads and candidate appearances on statewide presidential votes, 1988-96. *American Political Science Review, 93*, 345–362.

Shaw, D. R. (1999b). A study of presidential campaign event effects from 1952 to 1992. *Journal of Politics, 61*, 387–422.

*Shen, I., & Benoit, W. L. (2016). 2012 presidential campaign and social media: A Functional Analysis of candidates' Facebook public pages. *Midsouth Political Science Review, 17*, 53–80.

Sides, J., & Vavreck, L. (2013). The gamble: Choice and chance in the 2012 presidential election. Princeton, NJ: Princeton University Press.

Skewes, E. A. (2007). *Message control: How news is made on the campaign trail.* Lanham, MD: Rowman & Littlefield.

Smith, C. A. (2005). Candidate strategies in the 2004 presidential campaign: Instrumental choices faced by the incumbent and his challengers. In R. E. Denton (Ed.), *The 2004 presidential campaign: A communication perspective* (pp. 131–151). Lanham, MD: Rowman & Littlefield.

Smith, C. A., & Mansharamani, N. (2002). Challenger and incumbent reversal in the 2000 election. In R. E. Denton (Ed.), *The 2004 presidential campaign: A communication perspective* (pp. 91–116). Westport, CT: Praeger.

Stewart, C. J. (1975). Voter perception of mud-slinging in political communication. *Central States Speech Journal, 26*, 279–286.

Sullivan, J., & Sapir, E. V. (2012). Modeling negative campaign advertising: Evidence from Taiwan. *Asian Journal of Communication, 22*, 289–303.

Thorson, E., Christ, W. G., & Caywood, C. (1991). Effects of issue-image strategies, attack and support appeals, music, and visual content in political commercials. *Journal of Broadcasting and Electronic Media, 35*, 465–486.

Trent, J. D., & Trent, J. S. (1995). The incumbent and his challengers: The problem of adapting to prevailing conditions. In K. E. Kendall (Ed.), *Presidential campaign discourse: Strategic communication problems* (pp. 69–93). Albany, NY: State University of New York Press.

Trent, J. S., & Trent, J. D. (1974). The rhetoric of the challenger: George Stanley McGovern. *Central States Speech Journal, 25*, 11–18.

Wanat, J. (1974). Political broadcast advertising and primary election voting. *Journal of Broadcasting, 18*, 413–422.

Washington Post. (2016). Money raised as of October 19. Accessed 11/6/16: https://www.washingtonpost.com/graphics/politics/2016-election/campaign-finance/

West, D. M. (2001). *Air wars: Television advertising in election campaigns, 1952-2000* (3rd ed.). Washington, DC: Congressional Quarterly.

Wolf, F. M. (1986). *Meta-analysis: Quantitative methods for research synthesis.* Beverly Hills, CA: Sage Publications.

Wilson, R. (2012, November 2). Obama and Romney teams top $1 billion in ad spending: The Romney side is outspending Obama, and both sides are now emptying their coffers at an unprecedented pace. *National Journal.* Accessed 3/31/13: http://www.nationaljournal.com/politics/obama-and-romney-teams-top-1-billion-in-ad-spending-20121102

*Designates a study contributing data to the meta-analysis.

The authors would like to thank *Delta Sigma Rho-Tau Kappa Alpha*, *Speaker & Gavel*, and Todd Holm for permission to reprint this essay.

References

Abramowitz, A. I., & Webster, S. W. (2016). The rise of negative partisanship and the nationalization of US elections in the 21st century. *Electoral Studies*, *41*, 12–22.

Abramowitz, A. I., & Webster, S. W. (2018). Negative partisanship: Why Americans dislike parties but behave like rabid partisans. *Advances in Political Psychology*, *39*, 119–135.

Abramson, A. (2016, December 22). Hillary Clinton wins popular vote by nearly 2.9 million. *ABCNews*. Accessed 7/23/18: https://abcnews.go.com/Politics/hillary-clinton-officially-wins-popular-vote-29-million/story?id=44354341

Airne, D., & Benoit, W. L. (2005). Political television advertising in campaign 2000. *Communication Quarterly*, *53*, 473–493.

Anderson, M. (2015). More Americans are using social media to connect with politicians. *Pew Research Center*. Accessed 8/1/16: http://www.pewresearch.org/fact-tank/2015/05/19/more-americans-are-using-social-media-to-connect-with-politicians/

Auter, Z. J., & Fine, J. A. (2016). Negative campaigning in the social media age: Attack advertising on Facebook. *Political Behavior*, *38*, 999–1020.

Baker, K. L., & Norpoth, H. (1981). Candidates on television: The 1972 electoral debates in West Germany. *Public Opinion Quarterly*, *45*, 329–345.

Balz, D. (2012, July 29). 8 questions. *The Washington Post*. Accessed 12/10/13 http://www.washingtonpost.

Beevolve. (2017). An exhaustive study of Twitter users across the world. Accessed 2/17/17: http://www.beevolve.com/twitter-statistics

Benoit, W. L. (2000). A Functional Analysis of political advertising across media, 1998. *Communication Studies*, *51*, 274–295.

Benoit, W. L. (2003). Topic of presidential campaign discourse and election outcome. *Western Journal of Communication*, *67*, 97–112.

Benoit, W. L. (2004). Political party affiliation and presidential campaign discourse. *Communication Quarterly*, *52*, 81–97.

Benoit, W. L. (2006). Retrospective versus prospective statements and outcome of presidential elections. *Journal of Communication*, *56*, 331–345. DOI: 10.1111/j.1460-2466.2006.00022.x.

Benoit, W. L. (2007). *Communication in political campaigns*. New York: Peter Lang.

Benoit, W. L. (2013). Mudslinging: The nature of attacks in political campaigns. In C. Rountree (Ed.), *Venomous speech and other problems in American political discourse* (pp. 129–147). Westport, CT: Praeger.

Benoit, W. L. (2014a). *A functional analysis of political television advertisements* (2nd ed.). Lanham, MD: Lexington Books.

Benoit, W. L. (2014b). A Functional analysis of 2008 and 2012 presidential nomination acceptance addresses, *Speaker & Gavel*, *51*, 50–59.

Benoit, W. L. (2014c). *Political election debates: Informing voters about policy and character*. Lanham, MD: Lexington Books.

Benoit, W. L. (2015). Functional Theory: Negative campaigning in political TV spots. In A. Nai & A. Walter (Eds.). *New perspectives on political campaigning: Why attack politics matter* (pp. 35–46). Colchester, England: European Consortium for Political Research Press.

Benoit, W. L. (2017a). The Functional Theory of political campaign discourse. In R. E. Denton (Ed.), *Political campaign communication: Theory, method and practice* (pp. 3–32). Lanham, MD: Lexington.

Benoit, W. L. (2017b). Meta-analysis of research on the Functional Theory of Political Campaign Discourse. *Speaker & Gavel*, *54*, 7–50.

Benoit, W. L., Blaney, J. R., & Pier, P. M. (1998). *Campaign '96: A functional analysis of acclaiming, attacking, and defending*. New York: Praeger.

Benoit, W. L., & Glantz, M. (2013). A Functional analysis of 2008 and 2012 presidential candidacy announcement speeches. *Speaker & Gavel*, *50*, 47–62.

Benoit, W. L., & Glantz, M. (2015). A Functional Analysis of 2012 United States general election presidential and vice presidential debates. In C. Beiber & K. Kamps (Eds.), *Die US-Prasidentschaftswahl* (pp. 289–306). Wiesbaden: Springer Fachmedien.

Benoit, W. L., & Glantz, M. (2017). *Persuasive attack on Donald Trump in the 2016 Republican primaries*. Lanham, MD: Lexington Books.

Benoit, W. L., Glantz, M., & Rill, L. (2016). Campaigning on the Internet: 2008 presidential general election candidate webpages. *KOME: An International Journal of Communication Inquiry*, *4*, 46–58.

Benoit, W. L., Hansen, G. J., & Verser, R. M. (2003). A meta-analysis of the effects of viewing U.S. presidential debates. *Communication Monographs*, *70*, 335–350. DOI: 10.1080/03637 75032000179133.

Benoit, W. L., Henson, J., Davis, C., Glantz, M., Phillips, A., & Rill, L. (2013). Stumping on the Internet: 2008 presidential primary candidate campaign webpages. *Human Communication*, *16*, 1–12.

Benoit, W. L., Henson, J. R., & Sudbrock, L. A. (2011). A functional analysis of 2008 U.S. presidential primary debates. *Argumentation and Advocacy, 48*, 97–110.

Benoit, W. L., Henson, J., Whalen, S., & Pier, P. M. (2008). "I am a candidate for president": A functional analysis of presidential announcement speeches, 1960-2004. *Speaker & Gavel, 45*, 3–18.

Benoit, W. L., McHale, J. P, Hansen, G. J., Pier, P. M., & McGuire, J. P. (2003). *Campaign 2000: A functional analysis of presidential campaign discourse.* Lanham, MD: Rowman & Littlefield.

Benoit, W. L., Leshner, G. M., & Chattopadhyay, S. (2007). A meta-analysis of political advertising. *Human Communication, 10*, 507–522.

Benoit, W. L., Pier, P. M., Brazeal, L. M., McHale, J. P., Klyukovksi, A., & Airne, D. (2002). *The primary decision: A functional analysis of debates in presidential primaries.* Westport, CT: Praeger.

Benoit, W. L., & Stein, K. A. (2018). *The use of Twitter in 2016 non-presidential campaigns.* National Communication Association, Salt Lake City, UT.

Benoit, W. L., Stein, K. A., McHale, J. P., Chattopadhyay, S., Verser, R., & Price, S. (2007). *Bush versus Kerry: A functional analysis of campaign 2004.* New York: Peter Lang.

Benoit, W. L., Wells, W. T., Pier, P. M., & Blaney, J. R. (1999). Acclaiming, attacking, and defending in presidential nomination convention acceptance addresses, 1960-1996. *Quarterly Journal of Speech, 85*, 247–267. DOI: 10.1080/00335639909384260.

Borah, P. (2016). Political Facebook use: Campaign strategies used in 2008 and 2012 presidential elections. *Journal of Information Technology & Politics, 13*, 1–13.

Borrell Associates. (2017, January 3). The final analysis: Political advertising in 2016. Accessed 1/6/16: https://www.borrellassociates.com/industry-papers/papers/2016/the-final-analysis-political-advertising-in-2016-detail

Bramlett, J. C., McKinney, M. S., & Warner, B. R. (2018). Processing the political: Presidential primary "live-tweeting" as information processing. In B. R. Warner, D. G. Bystrom, M. S. McKinney, & M. C. Banwart (Eds.), *An unprecedented election: Media, communication and the electorate in the 2016 campaign* (pp. 169–188). Santa Barbara, CA: Praeger.

Brazeal, L. M., & Benoit, W. L. (2001). A functional analysis of congressional television spots, 1986-2000. *Communication Quarterly, 49*, 436-454.

...al, L. M., & Benoit, W. L. (2006). On the spot: A functional analysis of congressional ... 1980-2004. *Communication Studies, 57*, 401-420.

...*utation, image and impression management.* Chichester: Wiley.

... February 10). Is Donald Trump self-funding his campaign? Sort of. ...18: http://www.politifact.com/truth-o-meter/statements/2016/ ...-trump-self-funding-his-campaign-sort/

...son social media report. *Nielson.* Accessed 2/16/17: http:// .../reports/2017/2016-nielsen-social-media-report.html

..., February 4). The art of the presidential announcement, ... *News.* Accessed 6/25/18: https://abcnews.go.com/Politics/ ...t-lincoln-obama/story?id=28699010

Clinton, H. (2016, July 28). Full text: Hillary Clinton's DNC speech. *Politico*. Accessed 7/29/16: http://www.politico.com/story/2016/07/full-text-hillary-clintons-dnc-speech-226410

Collins, E. (2016, August 31). Poll: Clinton, Trump most unfavorable candidates ever. *USA Today*. Accessed 10/31/16: http://www.usatoday.com/story/news/politics/onpolitics/2016/08/31/poll-clinton-trump-most-unfavorable-candidates-ever/89644296/

Davenport, D. (2017, December 13). A growing cancer on Congress: The curse of party-line voting. *Forbes*. Accessed 9/14/18: https://www.forbes.com/sites/daviddavenport/2017/12/13/a-growing-cancer-on-congress-the-curse-of-party-line-voting/#22b69cb86139

Dudek, P., & Partacz, S. (2009). Functional theory of political discourse. Televised debates during the parliamentary campaign in 2007 in Poland. *European Journal of Communication*, *2*, 361-379.

Estimated cost of ads aired for 2016 U.S. presidential election, by candidate as of May, 2016 (in million U.S. dollars). (2016). *Statista*. Accessed 7/23/18: http://www.statista.com/statistics/564155/cost-estimate-of-ads-aired-2016-us-presidential-election-by-candidate/

Fishbein, M., & Ajzen, I. (2010). *Predicting and changing behavior: The reasoned action approach*. New York: Psychology Press.

Gainous, J., & Wagner, K. M. (2014). *Tweeting to power: The social media revolution*. Oxford: Oxford University Press.

Geer, J. G. (2006). *In defense of negativity: Attack ads in presidential campaigns*. Chicago, IL: University of Chicago Press.

Glantz, M., & Benoit, W. L. (2018). The world's all atwitter: Image repair discourse on social media. In L. Austin & Y. Jin (Eds.), *Social media and crisis communication*. New York: Routledge.

Glantz, M., Benoit, W. L., & Airne, D. (2013). A Functional Analysis of 2012 U.S. presidential primary debates. *Argumentation and Advocacy*, *49*, 275–285.

Grynbaum, M. M. (2016, September 27). At 84 million viewers, debate was the most-watched ever. *New York Times*. Accessed 6/23/19: https://www.nytimes.com/2016/09/28/business/media/at-nearly-84-million-viewers-debate-may-be-the-most-watched-ever.html

History of Facebook. (2017). *Wikipedia*. Accessed 2/14/17: https://en.wikipedia.org/wiki/History_of_Facebook

History of the Internet. (2016). *Wikipedia*. Accessed 4/12/16: https://en.wikipedia.org/wiki/History_of_the_Internet

Hofstetter, C. R. (1976). *Bias in the news: Network television coverage of the 1972 election campaign*. Columbus, OH: Ohio State University Press.

Holbrook, T. M. (1995). *Do campaigns matter?* Thousand Oaks, CA: Sage.

Hrbkova, L., & Zagrapan, J. (2014). Slovak political debates: Functional theory in a multi- system." *European Journal of Communication*, *29*, 735-744.

Huddleston, T. (2016, July 29). More people watched Donald Trump's RNC speech Clinton's *Fortune*. Accessed 6/24/19: http://fortune.com/2016/07/29/rnc-d

Ingraham, C. (2017, April 14). Somebody just put a price tag on the 201 doozy. *Washington Post*. Accessed 6/23/18: https://www.washin wonk/wp/2017/04/14/somebody-just-put-a-price-tag-on-the- doozy/?noredirect=on&utm_term=.f0e62543cdcb

Internet Live Stats. (2017). *InternetLiveStats.* Accessed 2/14/17: http://www.internetlivestats.com/

Isotalus, P. (2011). Analyzing presidential debates: Functional theory and Finnish political communication culture. *Nordicom Review, 1,* 31-43.

Jarman, J. W. (2005). Political affiliation and presidential debates: A real-time analysis of the effect of the arguments used in the presidential debates. *American Behavioral Scientist, 49,* 229–242.

Kaye, K. (2017, January 3). Data-driven targeting creates huge 2016 political ad shift: Broadcast TV down 10%, cable and digital way up. *AdAge.* Accessed 6/2/18: http://adage.com/article/media/2016-political-broadcast-tv-spend-20-cable-52/307346/

Kig, A. (2002). Conclusions and implications. In A. King (Ed.), *Leaders' personalities and the outcomes of democratic elections* (pp. 210-221). Oxford: University Press.

Knapton, S. (2016, January 20). Facebook users have 155 friends. *Telegraph.* Accessed 2/17/17: http://www.telegraph.co.uk/news/science/science-news/12108412/Facebook-users-have-155-friends-but-would-trust-just-four-in-a-crisis.html

Koblin, J. (2016, October 20). Tumultuous debate draws over 71 million viewers. *New York Times.* Accessed 6/23/119: https://www.nytimes.com/2016/10/21/business/media/presidential-debate-third-70-million-viewers.html

Kreig, G. (2016, December 22). It's official: Clinton swamps Trump in the popular vote. *CNN.* Accessed 6/2/18: https://www.cnn.com/2016/12/21/politics/donald-trump-hillary-clinton-popular-vote-final-count/index.html

Kurtz, H. (2008, April 18). Performance by ABC.s moderators is a matter of debate. *The Washington Post,* p. C1.

Landis, J. R., & Koch, G. G. (1977). The measurement of observer agreement for categorical data. *Biometrica, 33,* 159–174.

Lanoue, D. J. (1994). Retrospective and prospective voting in presidential year elections. *Political Research Quarterly, 47,* 193–205.

Lawless, J. (2012). *Becoming a candidate.* Cambridge: Cambridge University Press.

Lee, C., & Benoit, W. L. (2005). A functional analysis of the 2002 Korean presidential debates. *Asian Journal of Communication, 15,* 115-132.

Lichterman, J. (2015, July 14). New Pew data: More Americans are getting news on Facebook and Twitter. *Nieman Lab.* Accessed 8/1/16: http://www.niemanlab.org/2015/07/new-pew-data-more-americans-are-getting-news-on-facebook-and-twitter/

Memmott, M., & Carnia, C. (2007, November 28). GOP presidential candidates to go another round. *USA Today,* p. 5A.

Merritt, S. (1984). Negative political advertising: Some empirical findings. *Journal of Advertising, 13,* 27–38.

Nai, A., & Walter, A. S. (2015). The war of words: The art of negative campaigning. In A. Nai & A. S. Walter (Eds.), *New perspectives on negative campaigning: Why attack politics matter* (pp. 3–33). Colchester: ECPR.

Neville-Shepard, R. (2014). Presidential campaign announcements: A third-party variant. *Southern Communication Journal, 79,* 130–146.

Nielson. (2016, March 17). Are Americans watching the Republican or Democratic debates—or both? *Nielson Insights*. Accessed 6/22/19: https://www.nielsen.com/us/en/insights/article/2016/are-americans-watching-the-republican-or-democratic-debates-or-both/

Norrander, B. (2000). *Candidate attrition during the presidential nominating system*. Paper presented at the Joan Shorenstein Center on the Press, Politics, and Public Policy Roundtable, Harvard University. Cited in Patterson (2003) p. 228n.

Page, S. (2008, April 14). Democrat debates: One year later it's Clinton vs. Obama. *USA Today*, p. 6A.

Patterson, T. E. (2003). *The vanishing voter: Public involvement in an age of uncertainty*. New York: Random House.

Pew Research Center. (2015). Social networking use. Accessed 8/1/16: http://www.pewresearch.org/data-trend/media-and-technology/social-networking-use/

Pew Research Center. (2016). Election 2016: Campaigns as a direct source of news. Accessed 8/1/16: http://www.journalism.org/files/2016/07/PJ_2016.07.18_election-2016_FINAL.pdf

Pew Research Center. (2017, January 12). Social media fact sheet. Accessed 2/15/17: http://www.pewinternet.org/fact-sheet/social-media/

Political positions of Donald Trump. (2018). *Wikipedia*. Accessed 12/7/18: https://en.wikipedia.org/wiki/Political_positions_of_Donald_Trump

Reinemann, C., & Maurer, M. (2005). Unifying or polarizing? Short-term effects and post-debate consequences of different rhetorical strategies in televised debates. *Journal of Communication*, *55*, 775–794.

Rountree, J. C. (1995). The president as God, the recession as evil: *Actus*, *status*, and the president's rhetorical bind in the 1992 election. *Quarterly Journal of Speech*, *81*, 325–352.

Shen, I., & Benoit, W. L. (2016). 2012 presidential campaign and social media: A Functional analysis of candidates' Facebook public pages. *The Midsouth Political Science Review*, *17*, 53–82.

Stelter, B. (2015, December 16). GOP debate drew 18 million, third most-watched ever. *CNN*. Accessed 6/23/19: https://money.cnn.com/2015/12/16/media/gop-debate-ratings/index.html

Stewart, C. J. (1975). Voter perception of mud-slinging in political communication. *Central States Speech Journal*, *26*, 279–286.

Tani, M. (2015, September 10). Nate Silver: "Calm down," Trump won't win the GOP nomination. *Business Insider*. Accessed 6/2/18: http://www.businessinsider.com/nate-silver-donald-trump-wont-win-2015-9

Tankersley, J. (2015, October 20). The math is clear: Hillary Clinton has better odds of becoming president than anybody else – by far. *The Washington Post*. Accessed 6/2/18: https://www.washingtonpost.com/news/wonk/wp/2015/10/20/the-math-is-clear-hillary-clinton-has-better-odds-of-becoming-president-than-anybody-else-by-far/?noredirect=on&utm_term=.f3197a9d05dd

The Economist. (2016, December 28). America's electoral college and the popular vote: In America, winning the popular vote doesn't always lead to the White House. Accessed 7/23/18: https://www.economist.com/graphic-detail/2016/12/28/americas-electoral-college-and-the-popular-vote

Todd, C., & Murray, M. (2015, June 22). Jeb Bush surges to lead GOP pack in new 2016 poll. *MSNBC*. Accessed 6/2/18: http://www.msnbc.com/msnbc/jeb-bush-surges-lead-gop-pack-new-2016-poll

Trent, J. S. (1978). Presidential surfacing: The ritualistic and crucial first act. *Communication Monographs*, *45*, 281–292.

Trent, J. S. (1994). The early campaign. In R. E. Denton (Ed.), *The 1992 presidential campaign: A communication perspective* (pp. 43–64). New York: Praeger.

Trent, J. S. (1998). The beginning and the early end. In R. E. Denton (Ed.), *The 1996 presidential campaign: A communication perspective* (pp. 50–75). New York: Praeger.

Trent, J. S., & Friedenberg, R. V. (2004). *Political campaign communication: Principles and practices* (5th ed.). Westport, CT: Praeger.

Trump, D. (2016, July 21). Full Text: Donald Trump's 2016 Republican National Convention speech. *ABC*. Accessed 7/22/16: http://abcnews.go.com/Politics/full-text-donald-trumps-2016-republican-national-convention/story?id=40786529

Walter, A. S., & Nai, A. (2015). Explaining the use of attack behaviour in the electoral battlefield: A literature overview. In A. Nai & A. S. Walter (Eds.), *New perspectives on negative campaigning: Why attack politics matters* (pp. 99–113). Colchester: European Consortium for Political Research.

60 Minutes. (2017, October 8). Facebook "embeds," Russia and the Trump campaign's secret weapon: Brad Parscale, digital director for Trump's campaign, was a critical factor in the president's election. Now questions surround how he did it. Accessed 7/18/18: https://www.cbsnews.com/news/facebook-embeds-russia-and-the-trump-campaigns-secret-weapon/

Index

A

B

C

D

E

F

G

H

I

J

N

O

P

Q

R

S

T

U

V

W

Z

www.ingramcontent.com/pod-product-compliance
Ingram Content Group UK Ltd.
Pitfield, Milton Keynes, MK11 3LW, UK
UKHW020209290926
15470UKWH00001B/82

9 781433 168222